Level
3

Introduction to Academic Writing

THIRD EDITION

Alice Oshima
Ann Hogue

PEARSON
Longman

Introduction to Academic Writing, Third Edition

Pearson Education, 10 Bank Street, White Plains, NY 10606

Staff credits: The people who made up the *Introduction to Academic Writing* team, representing editorial,
    production, design, and manufacturing, are: Rhea Banker, Wendy Campbell, Elizabeth Carlson, Gina DiLillo,
    Christine Edmonds, Laura Le Dréan, Linda Moser, and Edith Pullman.
Cover design: Jill Lehan
Cover images: (left) Gianni Dagli Orti/Corbis. (right) Computer circuit board, close-up (digital composite) by
    Jan Franz. Collection: Stone. Getty Images.
Text composition: Integra
Text font: 11.5/13 Times Roman
Illustrator credits: Steve Attoe (29, 81, 95, 99, 114); Steve Schulman (108)
Photo credits: p. 1 Gianni Dagli Orti/Corbis; **p. 2** Image Source/Alamy; **p. 10** Ethan Miller/Reuters/Corbis;
    p. 23 Roger Ressmeyer/Corbis; **p. 26** Robert van der Hilst/Corbis; **p. 37** Tomi/Photolink/Getty Images;
    p. 48 Blickwinkel/Alamy; **p. 55** Birgid Allig/Getty Images; **p. 60** Elizabeth A. Whiting/Corbis; **p. 67** Rollie
    Rodriguez/Alamy; **p. 76** Andrew Fox/Corbis; **p. 86** Royalty-Free/Corbis; **p. 94** Tom Stewart/Corbis;
    p. 103 Bettmann/Corbis; **p. 108** TRBfoto/Getty Images; **p. 122** (left) Tom & Dee Ann McCarthy/Corbis;
    p. 122 (right) WorldFoto/Alamy; **p. 125** Jerry Pinkney/National Geographic Image Collection;
    p. 129 Paul Almasy/Corbis; **p. 140** Bettmann/Corbis; **p. 145** Bettmann/Corbis; **p. 146** Martin Philbey/
    ZUMA/Corbis; **p. 168** M. Thomsen/zefa/Corbis

Library of Congress Cataloging-in-Publication Data
Hogue, Ann.
    Introduction to academic writing/Ann Hogue, Alice Oshima. — 3rd ed.
      p.   cm.
    Includes index.
    ISBN 0-13-193395-7 (student book : alk. paper) — ISBN 0-13-241028-1 (answer key : alk. paper)
    1. English language—Rhetoric—Handbooks, manuals, etc.   2. English language—Grammar—Handbooks,
    manuals, etc.   3. English language—Textbooks for foreign speakers.   4. Academic writing—Handbooks,
    manuals, etc.   5. Report writing—Handbooks, manuals, etc.
    I. Oshima, Alice. II.   Title.
    PE1408.O72 2007
    808'.042—dc22   2006025633

Printed in the United States of America
3 4 5 6 7 8 9 10—VHG—10 09 08 07

Contents

Preface

Introduction to Academic Writing, Third Edition, is an intermediate writing textbook/ workbook for English language learners in academic settings. It teaches rhetoric and sentence structure in a straightforward manner, using a step-by-step approach, high-interest models, and varied practices.

Students are guided through the writing process to produce well-organized, adequately developed paragraphs and essays. Explanations are simple, and numerous practices help students assimilate each skill.

The book contains ten chapters: Chapters 1–8 teach paragraphs, and Chapters 9 and 10 introduce the essay. Most chapters also teach sentence structure, starting with simple sentences and progressing through compound and complex sentences. The chapters also include instruction in the writing process and punctuation.

What's New in the Third Edition

Instructors familiar with the Second Edition will find several changes. We have made these changes in response to the comments of reviewers and teachers who have used the Second Edition over the years.

- Paragraph writing takes center stage in this edition. Following two introductory chapters on paragraph format and structure are six more chapters on the paragraph. Essays are introduced in the final two chapters. As a result, rhetorical instruction flows more sequentially from paragraph to essay.
- There are more paragraph modes: narration, description, logical division of ideas, process, definition, and comparison/contrast. Each is presented in its own chapter.
- The organization of individual chapters has been changed. The gap between prewriting and final draft has been closed.
- The challenging but important academic skill of summary writing is introduced early on, in Chapter 3, and opportunities to write summaries are sprinkled throughout the book.
- Models and practice items have been updated or replaced. Old favorites have been retained, sometimes in a different form.
- New Try It Out! exercises allow students to try out new skills informally, without the pressure of being graded on their efforts.
- Journal writing has been added as an option. Instructions and topic suggestions appear as Appendix A at the back of the book.
- There are separate worksheets for self-editing and peer editing.

Order of Lesson Presentation

Introduction to Academic Writing is intended to be covered in one fifteen-week semester, with classes meeting five hours a week. Chapters 1–6 should be taught in order because the sentence structures presented in these chapters are sequenced, moving from simple sentences through compound sentences to complex sentences.

For courses shorter than fifteen weeks, or for classes that are on the low end of the intermediate range, Chapters 7, 8, and/or 9 and 10 can be skipped. These chapters teach more advanced rhetorical forms (definition, comparison/contrast, opinion essays) and sentence structures (adjective clauses and appositives).

Organization of the Chapters

Most chapters contain three sections: Organization, Sentence Structure, and Writing. Others contain a fourth section on Capitalization, Punctuation, or Summary Writing.

Six appendices at the back of the book contain reference charts of editing symbols, connecting words, transition signals, and other writing aids.

Organization Sections

In the Organization sections in Chapters 1–8, students learn paragraph format, paragraph structure, and patterns of organization such as time order and logical division. Chapters 9 and 10 help students make the transition to essay writing.

An overview of the writing process appears in Chapter 1, using a recurring model on a topic similar to the writing assignment for that chapter. The prewriting technique of listing is taught in Chapter 1; other prewriting techniques (clustering, freewriting, and outlining) follow in subsequent chapters. Editing is practiced throughout the book.

Sentence Structure Sections

A good portion of each chapter provides students with opportunities to improve the structure of their sentences. Beginning with simple sentences in Chapter 1, students learn to form compound sentences and finally complex sentences of increasing difficulty.

Writing Sections

Each Writing section reviews the points covered in the chapter and also offers Skill Sharpeners. Skill Sharpeners reinforce previously mastered skills such as outlining, summary writing, and punctuation that students need in order to write well. They are flexible; Skill Sharpeners can be assigned at any time, for example, when an instructor needs to fill the last few minutes of a class meeting, or they can be used as quiz material.

The Writing Assignment for each chapter contains clear step-by-step instructions. Students are never left wondering how to begin or what to do next. Because students will have encountered the topic for many writing assignments in practice exercises earlier in the chapter, they will have thought about or discussed their topic before they tackle writing about it.

Alternative Writing Topics expand the choices for students and instructors.

Models

Students see several writing models in each chapter. Each Organization section is preceded by a model paragraph or essay that demonstrates the rhetorical form taught in that chapter. Similarly, each Sentence Structure section begins with a model that demonstrates both the rhetorical mode just taught and the sentence structures just ahead. In addition, many practice exercises serve double duty—as models and as exercises.

Questions on the Models

Following each model are Questions on the Model that focus the students' attention on specific elements in the paragraph. These questions either help students consolidate material taught in previous chapters or prepare students for the learning task ahead. For example, one question on the descriptive paragraph model asks students to underline descriptive words. Another question might ask students to identify the type of concluding sentence, to notice the kinds of details used to support the topic sentence, or to circle transition signals. Other questions may target sentence-building skills.

Writing Topics	The topics listed for each writing assignment are only suggestions. We encourage teachers to look for current news topics or for photographs and charts in newspapers and magazines on which to base writing assignments. A big challenge is to keep a topic small enough so that students develop it adequately.
In-Class Writing	Group prewriting and in-class writing of first drafts are especially helpful in the early stages because the instructor is available for immediate consultation. Also, the instructor can check to make sure everyone is on the right track. Pair and group collaboration is appropriate for prewriting and editing work; however, writing is essentially an individual task even when done in class.
Explanations and Examples	Intermediate students grasp points more easily by seeing several examples rather than by reading long explanations. Therefore, explanations are brief, and examples are numerous. Important information such as comma rules, charts of transition signals, and sentence "formulas" is boxed.
Practice Exercises	Each teaching point is accompanied by a variety of practice exercises, which progress from recognition exercises to controlled production to communicative Try It Out! practices. Try It Out! exercises allow students to experiment with new skills—both rhetorical and sentence structure—informally, without the pressure of being graded on their experiments.
	In addition, students have opportunities to practice editing. Some Editing Practices ask them to look for sentence errors such as comma splices or run-ons, and others target punctuation. Still others ask them to analyze a paragraph for rhetorical devices or to check a paragraph for unity.
Appendices	There are six appendices at the back of the book.

Appendix A   Journal Writing
Appendix B   Correction Symbols
Appendix C   Summary of Punctuation Rules
Appendix D   Kinds of Sentences and Master List of Connecting Words
Appendix E   Master Chart of Transition Signals
Appendix F   Peer-Editing and Self-Editing Worksheets; Scoring Rubrics

Journal Writing

Appendix A contains instructions and topic suggestions for journal writing. We urge teachers to introduce journal writing early in the term. Journal writing is particularly valuable for students at the intermediate level to develop writing fluency.

Editing Worksheets

Appendix F contains peer-editing and self-editing worksheets for each writing assignment. Instructors can use one or the other, or both, as they prefer. Peer editors can write their comments on the worksheet. Alternatively, each student can read his or her draft aloud in a small group of classmates and then elicit oral comments and suggestions by asking the checklist questions. The student who has read then records the group's suggestions on his or her own paper. Instructors can also respond to student writing by using the peer-editing checklist.

Scoring Rubrics

Two sample scoring rubrics appear near the beginning of Appendix F, one for paragraphs and one for essays. Their purpose is twofold: to show students how instructors might evaluate their writing and to suggest a schema for instructors to do so. Instructors are invited to photocopy the rubrics. Of course, the rubrics may be modified to suit individual assignments and individual preferences.

Answer Key   An Answer Key is available upon request from the publisher.

Acknowledgments

We feel very privileged to offer a third edition of our book and sincerely appreciate the contributions of the many people who have helped shape it. First and foremost, we thank Laura Le Dréan, our senior editor, who traveled countless miles and spent countless hours gathering feedback from users of the previous editions. We also owe a special debt to Caroline Gibbs of City College of San Francisco for permission to use her superb material on Journal Writing.

To the many students and teachers who took the time to offer suggestions, we extend our heartfelt thanks. We thank the following for their detailed comments: **Rudy Besikof**, UCSD Extension, San Diego, CA; **Mary Brooks**, Eastern Washington University, Cheney, WA; **J. Maxwell Couper**, Miami Dade College, Miami, FL; Darla Cupery, Hope International University, Fullerton, CA; **Rose Giambrone**, Norwalk Community College, Norwalk, CT; **Patty Heiser**, University of Washington, Seattle, WA; **Brian McDonald**, Glendale Community College, Pasadena, CA; **Susan Peterson**, Baruch College, CUNY, New York, NY; **Kathleen Reardan-Anderson**, Montgomery College, Rockville, MD; **Dana Watson**, Lansing Community College, Lansing, MI; **Terri Wells**, University of Texas, Austin, TX. We hope you recognize the many places where your advice improved the book.

The Paragraph

PART I

CHAPTER 1

Paragraph Format

What Is Academic Writing?

Academic writing is the kind of writing used in high school and college classes. Academic writing is different from creative writing, which is the kind of writing you do when you write stories. It is also different from personal writing, which is the kind of writing you do when you write letters or e-mails to your friends and family. Creative writing and personal writing are informal, so you may use slang, abbreviations, and incomplete sentences. However, academic writing is formal, so you should not use slang or contractions. Also, you should take care to write complete sentences and to organize them in a certain way.

Academic writing in English is probably different from academic writing in your native language. The words and grammar and also the way of organizing ideas are probably different from what you are used to. In fact, the English way of writing may seem clumsy, repetitive, and even impolite to you. Just remember that it is neither better nor worse than other ways; it is just different.

This book will help you learn and practice the format, sentence structure, and organization appropriate for academic writing. We will begin by studying the **paragraph**.

Organization

A **paragraph** is a group of related statements that a writer develops about a subject. The first sentence states the specific point, or idea, of the topic. The rest of the sentences in the paragraph support that point.

Paragraph Format

Follow the instructions after the model when you prepare assignments for this class. There are instructions for both handwritten and computer-written work.

When you handwrite a paper, make it look like this:

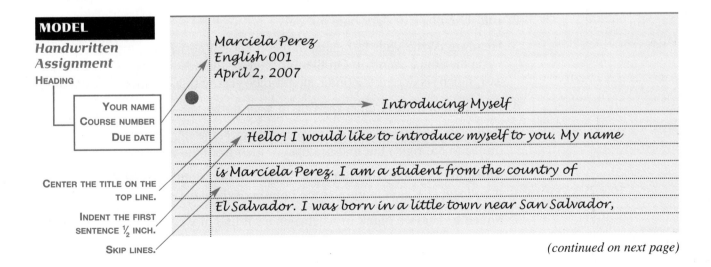

MODEL
Handwritten Assignment
HEADING

| YOUR NAME |
| COURSE NUMBER |
| DUE DATE |

CENTER THE TITLE ON THE TOP LINE.

INDENT THE FIRST SENTENCE ½ INCH.

SKIP LINES.

Marciela Perez
English 001
April 2, 2007

Introducing Myself

Hello! I would like to introduce myself to you. My name is Marciela Perez. I am a student from the country of El Salvador. I was born in a little town near San Salvador,

(continued on next page)

LEAVE 1-INCH MARGINS ON THREE SIDES.

←1″→   ←1″→

the capital of our country. I graduated from high school

there. I came to the United States two years ago with my

mother and my two sisters. We went to New York, where my

Uncle Eduardo lives. We lived with him and his family in their

house in Brooklyn for six months. He helped my sisters and me

get jobs. I work in a sweater factory. The factory is near City

College, where all of us take classes to learn English. Now we

have our own apartment. My sisters and I work during the day

and go to school at night. I want to quit my job in the factory

and go to school fulltime. I hope to go to college and become

a nurse-practitioner. I speak Spanish fluently. I don't think

I have any other special talents. My hobby is making jewelry.

I like to go to movies. That's all!

↑
1″
↓

1. **Paper** Use 8½-inch-by-11-inch lined, three-hole paper. The three holes should be on the left side as you write. Write on one side of the paper only.

2. **Ink** Use black or dark blue ink only.

3. **Heading** Write your full name in the upper left corner. On the next line, write the course number. On the third line of the heading, write the date the assignment is due in the order month-day-year with a comma after the day.

4. **Assignment Title** Center the title of your paragraph on the first line.

5. **Body** Skip one line, and start your writing on the third line. Indent (move to the right) the first sentence ½ inch from the left margin.

6. **Margins** Leave a 1-inch margin on the left and right sides of the paper. Also leave a 1-inch margin at the bottom of the page.

7. **Spacing** Leave a blank line between each line of writing.

When you type a paper on a computer, make it look like this:

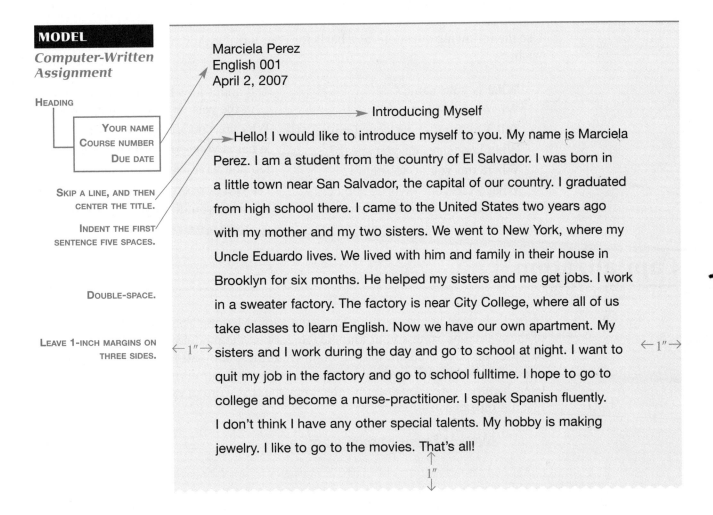

MODEL

Computer-Written Assignment

HEADING

> YOUR NAME
> COURSE NUMBER
> DUE DATE

SKIP A LINE, AND THEN CENTER THE TITLE.

INDENT THE FIRST SENTENCE FIVE SPACES.

DOUBLE-SPACE.

LEAVE 1-INCH MARGINS ON THREE SIDES.

Marciela Perez
English 001
April 2, 2007

Introducing Myself

Hello! I would like to introduce myself to you. My name is Marciela Perez. I am a student from the country of El Salvador. I was born in a little town near San Salvador, the capital of our country. I graduated from high school there. I came to the United States two years ago with my mother and my two sisters. We went to New York, where my Uncle Eduardo lives. We lived with him and family in their house in Brooklyn for six months. He helped my sisters and me get jobs. I work in a sweater factory. The factory is near City College, where all of us take classes to learn English. Now we have our own apartment. My sisters and I work during the day and go to school at night. I want to quit my job in the factory and go to school fulltime. I hope to go to college and become a nurse-practitioner. I speak Spanish fluently. I don't think I have any other special talents. My hobby is making jewelry. I like to go to the movies. That's all!

1. **Paper** Use 8½-inch-by-11-inch white paper.

2. **Font** Use a standard font, such as Times New Roman. Do not use underlining, italics, or bold type to emphasize words. It is not correct to do so in academic writing. Use underlining or italics only when required for titles of books and some other publications.

3. **Heading** Type your full name in the upper left corner ½ inch from the top of the page. On the next line, type the course number. On the third line of the heading, type the date the assignment is due in the order month-day-year with a comma after the day.

4. **Assignment Title** Skip one line, and then center your title. Use the centering icon on your word processing program.

5. **Body** Skip one line, and start typing on the third line. Use the TAB key to indent (move to the right) the first line of the paragraph. (The TAB key automatically indents five spaces.)

6. **Margins** Leave a 1-inch margin on the left and right.

7. **Spacing** Double-space the body.

Try It Out!   Write a paragraph 150 to 200 words long introducing yourself to your teacher and classmates. Use the model paragraph "Introducing Myself" as a guide. Make sure your paragraph is in the correct format.

Use the following questions as a basis for your writing. Add other information if you wish.

What is your name?

Where were you born?

Tell a little bit about your family.

What languages do you speak?

Where did you go to school?

What were your favorite subjects in school? Your least favorite?

Tell about jobs that you have had in the past or that you have now.

Why are you learning English?

What is your goal or your dream?

Do you have any special talents?

Do you have any hobbies?

What do you do in your free time?

Capitalization

In English there are many rules for using capital letters. You probably know many of them already. To test your knowledge, look at the model paragraph "Introducing Myself" on page 5 again. On the numbered lines, copy all the words or groups of words that begin with a capital letter. Add the capitalization rule, if you know it, next to each entry. *Note:* You don't need to copy the first word of every sentence or names that are repeated.

1. Marciela Perez—name of a person
2. _____
3. _____
4. _____
5. _____
6. _____
7. _____
8. _____
9. _____
10. _____
11. _____
12. _____
13. _____
14. _____
15. _____

Capitalization Rules

These are the most important rules for capitalization in English. Capitalize the following:

Rule	Example
1. The first word in a sentence	**M**y best friend is my dog.
2. The pronoun *I*	He and **I** never argue.
3. Abbreviations and acronyms formed from the first letters of words	**USA** **IBM** **AIDS** **UN** **VW** **CBS**
4. All proper nouns. Proper nouns include	
a. Names of deities	**G**od **A**llah **S**hiva
b. Names of people and their titles	**M**r. and **M**rs. **J**ohn **S**mith **P**resident **G**eorge **W**ashington
BUT NOT a title without a name	my math professor, the former prime minister
Note: Some writers capitalize titles such as *president* and *prime minister* when they clearly refer to one person	The president (OR President) will speak to the nation on television tonight.
c. Names of specific groups of people (nationalities, races, and ethnic groups), languages, and religions	**A**sian **J**apanese **M**uslim **C**aucasian **I**ndian **H**ispanic
d. Names of specific places on a map	**N**ew **Y**ork **C**ity **N**orth **P**ole **I**ndian **O**cean **M**ain **S**treet
e. Names of specific geographic areas	the **M**iddle **E**ast **E**astern **E**urope
BUT NOT the names of compass directions	Drive east for two blocks, and then turn south.
f. Names of days, months, and special days	**M**onday **I**ndependence **D**ay **J**anuary **R**amadan
BUT NOT the names of the seasons	spring, summer, fall (autumn), winter
g. Names of specific structures such as buildings, bridges, dams, monuments	**G**olden **G**ate **B**ridge **A**swan **H**igh **D**am the **W**hite **H**ouse **T**aj **M**ahal
h. Names of specific organizations (government agencies, businesses, schools, clubs, teams)	**S**tate **D**epartment **B**ank of **C**anada **H**arvard **U**niversity **N**ew **Y**ork **Y**ankees **F**rench **S**tudents **C**lub **R**ed **C**ross

(continued on next page)

Capitalization Rules   *(continued)*

Rule	Example	
i. Names of school subjects with course numbers	Business Administration 312 Chemistry 101	
BUT NOT names of classes without numbers, except languages	chemistry	French literature
j. First, last, and all important words in the titles of books, magazines, newspapers, plays, films, stories, songs, paintings, statues, television programs	*War and Peace* *Toronto Star* Jingle Bells	The Three Little Pigs *Paris Match* *Indiana Jones and* *The Temple of Doom*
Note: Italicize (or underline) titles of books, magazines, newspapers, plays, and films.		

PRACTICE I
Capitalization

A. In the following sentences, change small letters to capital letters where necessary.

1. farnaz is a student from iran. She speaks english, french, and farsi.

(F)   (I)   (E) (F) (F)

2. her major is business.

3. thanksgiving is a holiday in both canada and the united states, but it is celebrated on different days in the two countries.

4. it is celebrated on the fourth thursday in november in the united states and on the second monday in october in canada.

5. istanbul is a seaport city in turkey.

6. greenhills college is located in boston, massachusetts.

7. i am taking four classes this semester: american history, sociology 32, economics 40, and a computer science course.

8. i read a good book last weekend by ernest hemingway called *the old man and the sea.*

9. my roommate is from the south, so she speaks english with a southern accent.

10. the two main religions in japan are buddhism and shintoism.

B. Editing Practice   In the following paragraph, change small letters to capital letters wherever it is necessary.

a future businessman

i would like to introduce my classmate roberto sanchez. he is from the beautiful island of puerto rico in the caribbean sea. roberto is twenty-one years old. he was born in san juan, the capital city. his native language is spanish. he studied english in elementary school and in high school, too. roberto comes from a large family. he has three older brothers and two younger sisters. he likes to play the electric bass. he and some friends have a small band. sometimes they play on saturday nights at the fantasia club on fourth street in downtown san jose. baseball is his favorite sport. the san francisco giants are his favorite team. now he is studying english at greenhills college. in september of next year, he will begin to study business and computer science at a university. after graduation, he wants to work for a large tech company such as intel or ibm.

Try It Out!   Interview a classmate, using the questions from the Try It Out! exercise on page 6, or ask your own questions if you wish. (*Note*: Do not ask questions about age, religion, politics, or money. These subjects are very personal.) Then write a paragraph 150 to 200 words long introducing your classmate to the class. Focus on using capital letters correctly. Also focus on writing complete sentences.

What is your name?
Where were you born?
Tell a little bit about your family.
What languages do you speak?
Where did you go to school?
What were your favorite subjects in school? Your least favorite?

Tell about jobs that you have had in the past or that you have now.
Why are you learning English?
What is your goal or your dream?
Do you have any special talents?
Do you have any hobbies?
What do you do in your free time?

Sentence Structure

A Person Who Has Made a Difference: George Lucas

¹Filmmaker George Lucas has changed the film industry in many ways. ²He has written, directed, and produced some of the best-loved movies of our time. ³He has also made major contributions to modern film technology. ⁴At first, Lucas did not plan to become a filmmaker. ⁵His first dream was to become a race car driver. ⁶After a bad accident, however, he decided to go to college. ⁷In college, Lucas studied movie-making and made a number of student films. ⁸Lucas's third feature film, *Star Wars*, changed everything. ⁹A seemingly simple story of good versus evil, *Star Wars* became a huge international hit.¹ ¹⁰The movie used new technologies that revolutionized² the film industry. ¹¹One new technology was a special computer-assisted camera crane.³ ¹²Camera operators filmed most of the space fight scenes from the crane. ¹³Lucas is also responsible for the modern THX sound system, which improves the way a movie sounds in theaters. ¹⁴His latest innovation⁴ is the use of digital photography in filmmaking. ¹⁵To sum up, George Lucas's love of storytelling and his technological innovations have transformed⁵ movie-making forever.

Questions on the Model
1. In sentence 1, what is the subject? What is the verb? Underline the subject with one line and the verb with two lines.
2. In sentence 7, underline the subject with one line. How many verbs belong to this subject? Underline them with two lines.
3. In the last sentence of the paragraph, underline the verb with two lines. How many subjects are there? Underline them with one line.

---

¹**hit:** success
²**revolutionized:** completely changed
³**crane:** tall machine used to lift and move objects in the construction of buildings and to load and unload ships
⁴**innovation:** new idea or invention
⁵**transformed:** changed

Simple Sentences

A **sentence** is a group of words that (a) contains at least one subject and one verb and (b) expresses a complete thought.

There are four kinds of sentences in English: **simple sentences, compound sentences, complex sentences**, and **compound-complex sentences**. First, let's learn about simple sentences.

> A **simple sentence** has one subject-verb pair. The subject tells *who* or *what* did something. The verb tells the action (*jump, work, think*) or condition (*is, was, seem, appear*).
>
> Filmmaker George Lucas has changed the film industry in many ways.
>
> One new technology was a special computer-assisted camera crane.

A simple sentence can have one of several possible "formulas." Here are four possibilities. The subject(s) in each sentence are underlined with one line. The verb(s) are underlined with two lines.

		Sentence "formula"
1.	The *Star Wars* movies were international hits.	S V
2.	Young people and adults enjoyed them.	S S V
3.	The films entertained and thrilled audiences everywhere.	S V V
4.	Luke Skywalker and his friends battled evil and made us laugh at the same time.	S S V V

Notice that the subject in a simple sentence may have two or more items (sentences 2 and 4). The verb may have two or more items (sentences 3 and 4). These are all simple sentences because there is only one subject-verb pair.

Subject-Verb Agreement

You already know that subjects and verbs agree in number.

My sister **is** married. *(singular)*

My sisters **are** married. *(plural)*

My brother and I **are** single. *(plural)*

Subject-verb agreement is sometimes confusing in the following situations.

1. When a sentence begins with the word *there* + the verb *be*, the subject follows the *be* verb. Look ahead to see whether to use a singular or plural verb.

There **is a student** in the hall. *(The verb* is *is singular to agree with* a student.*)*
There **are three students** in the hall. *(The verb* are *is plural to agree with* three students.*)*

There **was no reason** for his action.
There **were many reasons** for his success.

2. A prepositional phrase (a group of words beginning with a preposition such as *of*, *with*, *in*, *at*, or *on* and ending with a noun or pronoun) can come between a subject and its verb. Prepositional phrases may come after a subject, but *they are not part of the subject.* You should mentally cross them out when you are deciding if the verb should be singular or plural.

> **One** (of my sisters) **is** a singer. *(The subject is* one, *not* sisters.*)*
> **The color** (of her eyes) **changes** when she is angry. *(The subject is* color, *not* eyes.*)*
> **Six kinds** (of rice) **are** available in the grocery store. *(The subject is* kinds, *not* rice.*)*

3. Some words are always singular.

> **One** (of my brothers) **is** a musician.
> **Neither** (of my parents) **is** living.
> **Much** (of my time) **is** spent in the library.
> **Each** (of my brothers) **wants** his own car.
> **Either** (of my sisters) **is** able to baby-sit for you tonight.
> **Nothing** ever **happens** in my life.
> **Is anyone** home?

4. A few words are always plural.

> **Both** (of my parents) **are** teachers.
> **Several** (of the teachers) **speak** my language.
> **Many** (of my friends) **work** in the library.

5. A few words can be either singular or plural. In these cases, you must refer to the noun in the prepositional phrase.

> **Some** (of the money) **was** missing. *(singular)*
> **Some** (of the students) **were** missing. *(plural)*
>
> **All** (of my time) **is** spent in the library. *(singular)*
> **All** (of my brothers) **are** singers. *(plural)*
>
> **Most** (of the ice) **was** melted. *(singular)*
> **Most** (of the ice cubes) **were** melted. *(plural)*
>
> **A lot** (of the work) **was** too easy. *(singular)*
> **A lot** (of the people) **were** angry. *(plural)*
>
> **None** (of the fruit) **is** fresh. *(singular)*
> **None** (of the apples) **are** fresh. *(plural)*

PRACTICE 2

*Identifying
Subjects, Verbs,
and Prepositional
Phrases*

Underline the subjects with one line and the verbs with two lines. Put parentheses ( ) around prepositional phrases.

1. <u>My name</u> <u><u>is</u></u> Roberto Sanchez.

2. <u>I</u> <u><u>was born</u></u> (on September 21, 1978,) (in the city) (of San Juan, Puerto Rico.)

3. I am a student at Greenhills College in Boston, Massachusetts.

4. Some of my classes are difficult.

5. Some of the homework is boring.

6. A lot of my classes are in Dante Hall.

7. A lot of my time is spent in the student lounge.

8. My father works in an office.

9. None of my brothers are married.

10. None of the money was stolen.

11. My youngest brother and sister are still in high school.

12. My father understands English but doesn't speak it.

13. In South America, most of the people are Catholic.

14. Neither of my parents has been to the United States.

PRACTICE 3

*Subject-Verb
Agreement*

A. In each sentence, underline the subject with one line and write S above it. Then cross out the incorrect verb form.

1. One of my classmates (is/~~are~~) from my country, El Salvador.

2. Some of the teachers (speak/speaks) my language.

3. Each of the gifts (was/were) carefully wrapped in gold paper.

4. One of the words on the test (was/were) misspelled.

5. A lot of my classes (was/were) canceled last week.

6. A lot of my time (is/are) spent in the library.

7. In my country most of the people (want to go/wants to go) to college.

8. (Do/Does) anyone know the correct time?

9. There (is/are) several kinds of flowers in the bouquet.

10. There (wasn't/weren't) any electricity in our building last night.

11. The noise from the firecrackers (was/were) loud.

B. Editing Practice   Find and correct six errors in subject-verb agreement in the following paragraph.

Young Golf Stars

[1]Golf is no longer the sport of rich, middle-aged, white men. [2]Young people around the world *are*[~~is~~] taking up[1] the game, and some of them *are*[~~is~~] taking it over.[2] [3]One of the young stars *is*[~~are~~] Sergio Garcia, a fascinating young golfer from Spain. [4]Sergio was born in 1980 and started playing golf at the age of 3. [5]He became a professional golfer in 1999 at the age of 19. [6]Sergio became famous by hitting a golf shot at a target from behind a tree with his eyes closed. [7]Two other young golf stars are Tiger Woods and Michelle Wie. [8]Both Tiger and Michelle started playing golf at very young ages, and both *have*[~~has~~] ethnic backgrounds. [9]Tiger, born in California in 1975, is Thai–African-American–Native-American. [10]Michelle, born in Hawaii in 1989, is Korean-American. [11]Each of these two young Americans *has*[~~have~~] shocked the world of golf in different ways. [12]Tiger shocked everyone by becoming the best golfer in the world while still in his early twenties. [13]Michelle shocked everyone by competing against men—and beating many of them—at the age of fourteen. [14]It is clear that all three of these young golfers *have*[~~has~~] great futures ahead of them.

Fragments

In some languages, you can sometimes leave out the subject in a sentence; in others, you can sometimes leave out the verb. In English, you must ALWAYS have at least one subject and one verb in every sentence.[3] If you leave out either the subject or the verb, your sentence is incomplete. We call an incomplete sentence a **fragment**.

These are fragments. Fragments are sentence errors.

> 1. Is not easy to get an A in Professor Wilson's class. *(There is no subject.)*
> 2. People in New York always in a hurry. *(There is no verb.)*

To correct Sentence 1, add a subject:

> **It** is not easy to get an A in Professor Wilson's class.

To correct Sentence 2, add a verb:

> People in New York **are** always in a hurry.

---

[1]**taking up:** learning
[2]**taking it over:** taking control over it
[3]There is one exception to this rule. In commands such as *Stop that!* and *Listen carefully*, the subject *you* is not expressed.

PRACTICE 4
Fragments

A. Step 1 Read each sentence and decide if it is a complete sentence or a fragment. Mark the fragments with an *X* to show that it is incorrect.

Step 2 Decide what is wrong with each fragment. Is the verb missing? Is the subject missing?

Step 3 Correct each fragment by adding a subject or a verb.

                     It is

__X__ 1. ~~Is~~ very hot today even with the windows open.

__X__ 2. Jose and Jin the smartest students in the class.

_____ 3. They study all the time.

__X__ 4. The baby finally sleepy.

_____ 5. She is closing her eyes.

__X__ 6. Ms. Woodbury, our grammar teacher, often late on Fridays.

__X__ 7. Is important for students to get to class on time.

B. Editing Practice Find and underline five fragments in the following paragraph. Then correct each one.

My Best Friend

    My best friend is Suzanne. We have been friends since childhood. As children we lived next door to each other in Caracas. Now live in different countries on different continents. She is married to a Venezuelan. Has three children. Her son two years old, and her twin daughters three months old. We haven't seen each other for eight years. We keep in touch by e-mail. Also telephone each other at least once a month. We will be friends forever.

The Writing Process

Overview

Writing is never a one-step action; it is an ongoing creative act. When you first write something, you have already been thinking about what to say and how to say it. Then after you have finished writing, you read over what you have written and make changes and corrections. You write and revise and write and revise again until you are satisfied that your writing expresses exactly what you want to say.

    The process of writing has roughly four steps. In the first step, you create ideas. In the second step, you organize the ideas. In the third step, you write a rough draft. In the final step, you polish your rough draft by editing it and making revisions.

Step 1: Prewriting

The first step is called *prewriting*. **Prewriting** is a way to get ideas. In this step, you choose a topic and collect ideas to explain the topic.

Listing There are several techniques you can use to get ideas. In this chapter, you will practice the technique called *listing*. **Listing** is a prewriting technique in which you write the topic at the top of a piece of paper and then quickly make a list of the words or phrases that come into your mind. Don't stop to wonder if an idea is good or not. Write it down! Keep on writing until the flow of ideas stops.

In the following example, the assignment was to write a paragraph about a person who has made a difference in the world, in the community, or in the writer's life.

First, the writer made a list of people who have made a difference. Then he decided which person to write about and circled his choice.

MODEL

Listing

A Person Who Has Made a Difference	
Albert Einstein	Bill Gates
Mother Teresa	Aunt Sarah
Martin Luther King, Jr.	Mr. Jakobsen (high school counselor)
Cesar Chavez	(Grandfather)

Next, the writer started a new list. He wrote his chosen topic, Grandfather, at the top of a new piece of paper and started writing words and phrases that came into his mind about his grandfather.

Grandfather	
uneducated (high school? eighth grade?)	started hospital in town — only hospital in big area
farmer	
worked hard	first farmer to terrace his land — now everyone does it
helped his community	
started community hospital	improved farming techniques in his area
respected in community	
went to church every week	smart
got up early	read about new things
worked late	terracing helps prevent soil erosion
was the first person in town to buy a car	listened to experts
	thought things over
forward-thinking	made me laugh when I was little

The writer then looked at his second list and decided to write about how his grandfather helped his community. He circled that idea. Then he thought about *how* his grandfather helped his community. He circled two ideas and marked them *A* and *B*. The writer also crossed out anything that didn't belong to these two ideas.

Grandfather

~~uneducated (high school? eighth grade?)~~   started hospital in town — only
~~farmer~~   hospital in big area
~~worked hard~~   first farmer to terrace his land —
(helped his community)   now everyone does it
B (started community hospital)   A (improved farming techniques
~~respected in community~~   in his area)
~~went to church every week~~   ~~read about new things~~
~~got up early~~   terracing helps prevent soil erosion
~~worked late~~   ~~listened to experts~~
~~was the first person in town~~   ~~thought things over~~
   ~~to buy a car~~   ~~made me laugh when I was little~~
~~forward-thinking~~

Try It Out!

Your writing assignment at the end of this chapter will be to write a paragraph about a person who has made a difference in the world, in his or her community, or in your life.

1. Use the listing technique to choose a person.
2. In a second list, write down the ways in which this person made a difference.
3. Choose one or two ways to write about, and circle them. (Do not write the paragraph yet.)

Step 2: Organizing

The next step in the writing process is to organize the ideas into a simple outline.

The writer of our models wrote a sentence that named the topic (his grandfather) and told the main idea (his grandfather helped his community). Below the first sentence, he listed the two main ideas and any other words and phrases from the list that gave more information about them.

MODEL

Simple Paragraph Outline

A Person Who Has Made a Difference: My Grandfather

My grandfather helped his community in two ways.

   A. He improved farming techniques in his area.

      • first farmer to terrace his land

      • terracing helps prevent soil erosion

   B. He started a community hospital.

      • only hospital in big area

Try It Out!   Make a simple outline from the lists you made in the Try It Out! exercise on page 17.

1. Give your outline a title like the one in the model.
2. Write a sentence like the one in the model that names the person and says what he or she did to make a difference.
3. Write the main idea(s) below this sentence. If there are two ideas as in the model, give them letters (*A* and *B*). If there is only one main idea, give a capital letter to every idea that you list below the first sentence.

Step 3: Writing

The next step is to write a rough draft, using your outline as a guide. Write your rough draft as quickly as you can without stopping to think about grammar, spelling, or punctuation. Just get your ideas down on paper. You will probably see many errors in your rough draft. This is perfectly usual and acceptable—after all, this is just a rough draft. You will fix the errors later.

Notice that the writer added some ideas that were not in his outline. Notice also that he added a concluding sentence at the end.

MODEL
Rough Draft

A Person Who Has Made a Difference: My Grandfather

My Grandfather help his community in two ways. My Grandfather born in 1880. He was farmer. Not well educated. (Maybe he only went to high school for one or two year. In those days, children were needed to work on the farm.) He was first farmer in his community to terrace his fields. Then, people thought he was crazy, but now, every farmer does it. Terracing helps prevent soil erosion. This improved farming techniques in his area. After he is too old to work at farming, my Grandfather get the idea that his town needs a Hospital, so he spend his time raising money to build one. There is no hospitals nearby, and people have to go long distance to see doctor. People again think he really crazy, but he succeed. Now a small Hospital in community, and two doctor. Each of the doctors have lots of patients. The Hospital is named the james walker community hospital. It was named for my Grandfather. My Grandfather just a simple, uneducated farmer, but he helped his community a lot.

Step 4: Polishing: Revising and Editing

In this step, you polish what you have written. This step is also called *revising and editing*. Polishing is most successful if you do it in two steps. First, attack the big issues of content and organization (**revising**). Then work on the smaller issues of grammar, punctuation, and mechanics (**editing**).

Peer Editing   On pages 198–207 are worksheets for each chapter to help you polish your writing. The first worksheet is for a peer editor to use. A peer editor is a classmate who reads your paper and helps you improve the content and organization.

A peer editor's job is to read, ask questions, and comment on what's good and on what might be changed or made clearer. He or she should not check your grammar or punctuation. Your instructor will help do this until you and your classmates learn to do it for yourselves.

In the following model, the peer editor's comments are on both sides of the page. The writer's replies are in blue. The writer and peer editor discuss the comments, and then the writer writes a second draft.

MODEL

Revising

A Person Who Has Made a Difference: My Grandfather

Good paragraph!

I especially like the part about the new hospital.

You use the word "crazy" a lot. Isn't it slang?
I can't think of a better word.

My Grandfather help his community in two ways. My Grandfather born in 1880. He was farmer. Not well educated. (maybe he only went to high school for one or two year. In those days, children were needed to work on the farm.) He was first farmer in his community to terrace his fields. Then, people thought he was crazy, but now, every farmer does it. Terracing helps prevent soil erosion. This improved farming techniques in his area. After he is too old to work at farming, my Grandfather get the idea that his town needs a hospital, so he spend his time raising money to build one. There is no hospitals nearby, and people have to go long distance to see doctor. People again think he really crazy, but he succeed. Now a small hospital in community, and two doctor. Each of the doctors have lots of patients. The hospital is named the james walker community hospital. It was named for my grandfather. My Grandfather just a simple, uneducated farmer, but he helped his community a lot.

I don't understand what "terracing" is. Please explain it. Also, what is "soil erosion"?

Are these sentences important? I don't think so.
You're right.

I don't think your grandfather would like this part!! ☺

MODEL
Second Draft

A Person Who Has Made a Difference: My Grandfather

My Grandfather help his community in two ways. He was farmer and lives in a small village. he was first farmer in his community to terrace his fields. Terracing is technique of making rows of little dams on hilly land. Terracing save water and keep soil from washing away in rainstorms. Then, people thought he was crazy, but now, all of the farmers in the area do it. Terracing helps keep the soil from washing away in rainstorms. This improved farming techniques in his area. then my Grandfather get the idea that his town need a Hospital, so he spend his time raising money to build one. There is no hospitals nearby, and people had to go long distance to see doctor. People again think he really crazy, but he succeed. Now a small Hospital in community, and two doctor. Each of the doctors have lots of patients. The Hospital is named the james walker community hospital. It was named for my Grandfather. My Grandfather just a simple, uneducated farmer, but he helped his community a lot.

Self-Editing   The other worksheet is for your use in revising and polishing your paper. This student writer checked his paper with the Self-Editing Worksheet, found and corrected most of his errors, and wrote the following final draft.

MODEL
Final Copy

A Person Who Has Made a Difference: My Grandfather

My grandfather helped his community in two ways. He was a farmer and lived in a small village. He was the first farmer in his community to terrace his fields. Terracing is the technique of making rows of little dams on hilly land. Terracing saves water and keeps soil from washing away in rainstorms. Then, people thought he was crazy, but now, all the farmers in the area do it. This improved farming techniques in his area. Then my grandfather got the idea that his town needed a hospital, so he spent his time raising money to build one. There were no hospitals nearby, and people had to go long distances to see a doctor. People again thought he was really crazy, but he succeeded. Now there is a small hospital in the community and two doctors. The hospital is named the James Walker Community Hospital. It was named for my grandfather. My grandfather was just a simple, uneducated farmer, but he helped his community a lot.

Review

These are the important points covered in this chapter:

1. Use correct format when preparing an assignment.

2. A sentence (a) has a subject and a verb and (b) expresses a complete thought.

3. A simple sentence has one subject-verb combination. A simple sentence may have more than one verb or more than one subject, but it has only one subject-verb *combination*.

4. Subjects and verbs always agree in number (singular or plural.) There are a few special situations that sometimes cause difficulties with subject-verb agreement.

5. A fragment is an incomplete sentence. It is a sentence error. A fragment might be missing a subject or a verb, or it might express an incomplete thought.

6. Know the rules for capitalization in English.

7. The process of writing has four main steps: prewriting, organizing, writing, and polishing.

   - Listing is a useful prewriting technique to get ideas.
   - Outlining is a good way to organize your ideas.

Writing Assignment

Choose a person who has made a difference in the world, in his or her community, or in your life. Write a paragraph of about 200 words about this person. Follow all the steps in the writing process.

Your classmates might be especially interested in learning about a person from your country, such as a politician, a sports star, a writer, an entertainer, and so on.

Step 1 Prewrite to get ideas. Use the listing practice that you completed in the Try It Out! exercise on page 17.

Step 2 Organize the ideas. Decide which idea will go first, second, third, and so on. Make a simple outline listing the ideas in the order you will write about them. Use the outline to guide you as you write.

Step 3 Write the rough draft. Write ROUGH DRAFT at the top of your paper.

- Begin your paragraph with a sentence that names the person and tells where or on whom he or she made a difference.

  My high school physics teacher changed my ideas about school.

  Martin Luther King, Jr. changed the way black people live in the United States forever.

- Pay attention to your sentence structure. Make sure all of your sentences have at least one subject and one verb.

Step 4 Polish the rough draft.

- Exchange papers with a classmate and ask him or her to check your rough draft using Peer-Editing Worksheet 1 on page 198. Then discuss the completed worksheet and decide what changes you should make. Write a second draft.
- Use Self-Editing Worksheet 1 on page 199 to check your second draft for grammar, punctuation, and sentence structure.

Step 5 Write a final copy. Hand in your rough draft, your second draft, your final copy, and the page containing the two editing worksheets. Your teacher may also ask you to hand in your prewriting paper.

Narrative Paragraphs

Organization
Time Order
Time Order Signals

Sentence Structure
Compound Sentences with *and*, *but*, *so*, and *or*

Punctuation
Three Comma Rules

The Writing Process
Freewriting

Review

Writing Assignment

Organization

Narration is story writing. When you write a narrative paragraph, you write about events in the order that they happen. In other words, you use **time order** to organize your sentences.

As you read the model paragraph, look for words and phrases that tell when something happened.

MODEL

Narrative Paragraph

Earthquake!

¹An unforgettable experience in my life was a magnitude 6.9 earthquake. ²I was at home with my older sister and younger brother. ³Suddenly, our apartment started shaking. ⁴At first, none of us realized what was happening. ⁵Then my sister yelled, "Earthquake! Get under something!" ⁶I half rolled and half crawled across the room to get under the dining table. ⁷My sister also yelled at my little brother to get under his desk. ⁸Meanwhile, my sister was on the kitchen floor holding her arms over her head to protect it from falling dishes. ⁹The earthquake lasted less than a minute, but it seemed like a year to us. ¹⁰At last, the shaking stopped. ¹¹For a minute or two, we were too scared to move. ¹²Then we tried to call our parents at work, but even our cell phone didn't work. ¹³Next, we checked the apartment for damage. ¹⁴We felt very lucky, for nothing was broken except a few dishes. ¹⁵However, our first earthquake was an experience that none of us will ever forget.

Questions on the Model
1. In which four sentences does the word *earthquake* appear?
2. What words and phrases show when different actions took place? Circle them.

Time Order

In the model **narrative** paragraph, the writer used **time order** to tell what happened first, what happened next, what happened after that, and so on.

Notice the kinds of words and phrases used to show time order. These are called *time order signals* because they signal the order in which events happen.

Time Order Signals

Words	Phrases
Finally,	At last,
First (second, third, etc.),	At 12:00,
Later,	After a while,
Meanwhile,	After that,
Next,	Before beginning the lesson,
Now	In the morning,
Soon	The next day,
Suddenly.	*At First*
Meanwhile	*At last.*
next.	*For a minute or two.*
then.	

Put a comma after a time order signal that comes before the subject at the beginning of a sentence. (Exception: *Then*, *soon*, and *now* are usually not followed by a comma.)

At first, none of us realized what was happening.

For a minute or two, we were too scared to move.

Then we tried to call our parents at work.

PRACTICE 1

Time Order

A. Look again at the model on page 24. Add any time order signal words or phrases that you circled to the Time Order Signals chart above.

B. Complete the paragraphs with time order signals from the lists provided, and capitalize and punctuate them correctly. Use each word or phrase once. There is more than one possible word or phrase to fill in some of the blanks.

1. Use these words and phrases:

first	after dinner
on the night before Thanksgiving	in the morning
about 3:00 in the afternoon	soon
then	before taking the first bite
after that	finally

Thanksgiving

Thanksgiving in the United States is a day for families to be together and enjoy a traditional meal. (a) <u>On the night before Thanksgiving,</u> our mother bakes a pumpkin pie, the traditional Thanksgiving dessert. (b) _____

___*First*_____ she gets up early to prepare the other traditional dishes.

In the morning

(continued on next page)

(c) _____ she makes dressing.[1] (d) _____ _____ she stuffs[2] the turkey with the dressing and puts the turkey into the oven to roast. (e) _____ she prepares the rest of the meal. She cooks all day long. (f) _____ _____ the family sits down at the table. (g) _____ _____ everyone around the table says one thing that they are thankful for. (h) _____ we can begin to eat. We stuff ourselves just as full as Mother stuffed the turkey earlier in the day! (i) _____ we are all groaning[3] because we have eaten too much. (j) _____ we collapse on the living room sofa and watch football games on TV. No one moves for at least two hours.

2. Use these words and phrases:

on the day of the party	first	next
during the party	after that	finally
before the party	then (use twice)	later
at the beginning of the party		

Fifteen Years

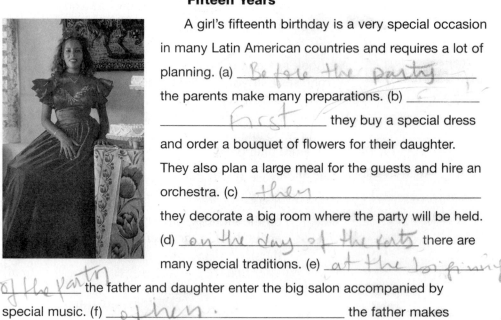

A girl's fifteenth birthday is a very special occasion in many Latin American countries and requires a lot of planning. (a) _Before the party_ the parents make many preparations. (b) _____ _____ First _____ they buy a special dress and order a bouquet of flowers for their daughter. They also plan a large meal for the guests and hire an orchestra. (c) _then_____ they decorate a big room where the party will be held. (d) _on the day of the party_ there are many special traditions. (e) _at the beginning of the party_ the father and daughter enter the big salon accompanied by special music. (f) _then._____ the father makes

_____

[1]**dressing:** mixture of bread cubes, onion, celery, butter, chicken broth, and herbs that is cooked inside a turkey. After it is cooked, it is removed from the turkey and eaten as a side dish. It is also called *stuffing*.
[2]**stuff:** put inside; fill until completely full
[3]**groaning:** making a long deep sound because you are in pain

a speech, and the daughter gets some presents. (g) _during the party_ everyone drinks champagne. (h) _next_ _____ the father and daughter dance a waltz, and the daughter and every boy dance one dance together. (i) _After that_ _____ all of the guests make a line to congratulate her. (j) _Later_ _____ all of the boys stand in a group because she will throw the bouquet, and the boy who catches it dances with her. (k) _Finally_ _____ everyone dances to different kinds of music until six o'clock in the morning.

C. The following sets of sentences are not in correct time order. Number the sentences in the correct order.

1. __6__ She put the clean dishes away.

    __2__ She removed the dirty dishes from the table.

    __5__ She turned on the dishwasher.

    __4__ She put them in the dishwasher.

    __3__ She piled them in the sink and rinsed them.

    __1__ It was Sarah's turn to wash the dishes last night.

    __7__ Finally, the dishes were clean.

2. __7__ He filled it out and left.

    __2__ He went to the bookshelf, but the book wasn't there.

    __1__ Tom went to the library to get a book.

    __3__ He went to the computer catalog.

    __6__ The librarian told him to fill out a form.

    __4__ He told the librarian he wanted to reserve that book.

    __5__ He wrote down the title and call number[4] of the book.

(continued on next page)

---

[4]**call number:** number written on the outside of a book; the book's "address" on the library shelves

3.

_6_ He gave us a room with an ocean view.

_3_ The airline had oversold[1] economy class seats, so we got to sit in first class.

_4_ Our good fortune continued at the hotel.

_x_ We can't wait to visit Florida again.

_7_ The hotel manager also gave us coupons for lots of free things.

_5_ The hotel manager apologized for not having our room ready when we arrived.

_1_ Our vacation in Florida last month was almost perfect.

_8_ The weather was warm and sunny, so we went to the beach every day.

_2_ Our good fortune began at the airport.

Try It Out!

Write the sentences from the preceding exercise as paragraphs. Try to make your paragraphs flow smoothly by using these two techniques: (1) Add time order signals at the beginning of some of the sentences. (2) Combine some of the sentences to form simple sentences with one subject and two verbs.

Example

It was Sarah's turn to wash the dishes last night. First, she removed the dirty dishes from the table. Next, she piled them in the sink and rinsed them. After that, she put them in the dishwasher and turned it on. Finally, the dishes were clean.

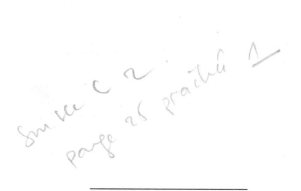

---

[1]**oversold:** sold more seats than were available

Sentence Structure

The model for this section is a folktale. A folktale is a traditional story that has been passed down orally from one generation to the next until someone finally writes it down. Every culture is rich in folktales. This one is from Japan.

MODEL

Compound Sentences

once upon a time.

Omusubi Kororin (The Tumbling Rice Balls)
A Folktale from Japan

¹Once upon a time, an old couple lived in the countryside. ²They were happy, but they were poor. ³One day, the old man went to work in the forest and took his usual lunch of three rice balls. ⁴During lunch, he dropped a rice

ball, and it rolled into a hole in the ground. ⁵He heard happy singing coming from the hole, so he dropped the other two rice balls into it. ⁶Inside the hole, some mice were having a party. ⁷They thanked him for the rice balls and invited him to join them. ⁸After a while, the mice told him to choose a box as a reward for his generosity.² ⁹He could choose a big box, or he could choose a small one. ¹⁰He thought about taking a big box, but he finally chose a small one. ¹¹Back at home, he and his wife discovered that the box was full of gold coins. ¹²A greedy³ neighbor heard about their good fortune and quickly made plans to visit the same hole. ¹³At the hole, he pushed several rice balls into it, and sure enough,⁴ the mice invited him in. ¹⁴The greedy man wanted all of the mice's gold, so he pretended to be a cat. ¹⁵He started meowing loudly, and the frightened mice ran away. ¹⁶The gold disappeared with the mice, so the greedy man got nothing, not even a rice ball.

Questions on the Model
1. What kind of order does this folktale use?
2. Circle the time order signals and add any new ones to the Time Order Signals chart on page 25.

---

²**generosity:** willingness to give money, time, help, and so on
³**greedy:** always wanting more money, possessions, power, and so on
⁴**sure enough:** informal expression that means something happens just as expected

Compound Sentences with *and*, *but*, *so*, and *or*

In Chapter 1, you learned about simple sentences. A simple sentence has one subject-verb combination. Another kind of sentence is a compound sentence. A compound sentence has two or more subject-verb combinations.

> A **compound sentence** is composed of at least two simple sentences joined by a comma and a coordinating conjunction. A compound sentence has this "formula":
>
> ```
>    ┌──S──┐ ┌────V────┐                         COORD.    ┌─────S─────┐ ┌─V─┐
>                                                CONJ.
>    The gold disappeared with the mice,          so       the greedy man got nothing.
> ```

There are seven coordinating conjunctions in English: *and*, *but*, *so*, *or*, *for*, *nor*, and *yet*. In this chapter, you will study the first four.[1]

Coordinating Conjunctions

Coordinating Conjunction	Example
And joins sentences that are alike.	He dropped a rice ball, **and** it rolled into a hole in the ground.
But joins sentences that are opposite or show contrast.	They were happy, **but** they were poor.
So joins sentences when the second sentence expresses the result of something described in the first sentence.	The greedy man wanted all of the mice's gold, **so** he pretended to be a cat.
Or joins sentences that give choices or alternatives.	He could choose a big box, **or** he could choose a small one.

Use a comma before a coordinating conjunction in compound sentences only. Do not use a comma to join two words or two phrases in a simple sentence.

COMPOUND SENTENCES (COMMA)

Yesterday we went shopping, but we didn't buy anything.
The stores were crowded, and they were noisy.
We ate lunch, and then we went home.

SIMPLE SENTENCES (NO COMMA)

Yesterday we went shopping but didn't buy anything.
The stores were crowded and noisy.
We ate lunch and then went home.

PRACTICE 2

Compound Sentences with and, but, so, *and* or

A. Draw a box around each coordinating conjunction in the story "Omusubi Kororin" on page 29. Explain why some of them have commas, but others don't.

B. Decide which of the following sentences are compound sentences and which are simple sentences. Write *CS* or *SS* on the line at the left. Then add commas to the compound sentences.

---

[1]Coordinating conjunctions are sometimes called *fan boys* because their first letters spell those words: **f**or, **a**nd, **n**or, **b**ut, **o**r, **y**et, and **s**o.

Monsieur Seguin's Goat
A Folktale from France

<u>SS</u>   1. A long time ago, high in the Alps, an old man lived with his goat, Blanchette.

_____   2. She was a wonderful white goat and was very kind to her master, Monsieur Seguin.

_____   3. They had lived together for many years.

_____   4. Blanchette was always fastened to a tree.

_____   5. She was often sad and sometimes she didn't eat her food.

_____   6. Every day, she looked at the big mountains and dreamed of being free to explore them.

_____   7. One day, she asked her master for more freedom.

_____   8. "You can tie me with a longer rope or you can build a special enclosure for me," said Blanchette.

_____   9. At first, he tied her with a longer rope but Blanchette was still sad.

_____ 10. A few days later, he built a special enclosure.

_____ 11. For a while, Blanchette was very happy about this decision but soon the enclosure seemed very small in front of the big mountains.

_____ 12. One summer morning, Blanchette decided to leave for the mountains so she jumped out of the enclosure and ran away.

_____ 13. "I am free," she said.

_____ 14. She ate many varieties of plants and enjoyed meeting new friends.

_____ 15. All day, she ran in the Alps.

_____ 16. Finally, the sun set behind the hills.

C. For each set of sentences, make a compound sentence or a simple sentence with two verbs. Use the coordinating conjunction *and*, *but*, *or*, or *so* to join the sentences. Punctuate carefully. There may be more than one way to combine some of the sentences.

   1. It became very dark. Blanchette was suddenly afraid.

    <u>It became very dark, and Blanchette was suddenly afraid.</u>

   2. She heard a noise. She decided to go back to her enclosure.

    _____

   3. She walked for a long time. She couldn't find the road.

    _____

(continued on next page)

4. Finally, she became very tired. She tried to rest. Her fear prevented her from sleeping. (Combine all three sentences.)

_____

5. Suddenly, a wolf appeared. The wolf looked at her hungrily.

_____

6. She shouted for help. No one heard her.

_____

7. The wolf ate Blanchette. The poor old man never saw his little goat again.

_____

8. Blanchette wanted to be free. Freedom can be dangerous when we disobey.

_____

D. On a separate piece of paper, write compound sentences using the coordinating conjunctions you have learned. Follow the directions given.

1. Write a sentence that tells one thing you like to do and one thing you don't like to do. (Use *but*.)

   Example: I like to swim in the ocean, but I don't like to swim in swimming pools.

2. Write a sentence that tells two things you do every morning after you get up. (Use *and*.)

3. Write a sentence that tells two things you might do during your next vacation. (Use *or*.)

4. Write a sentence that tells the results of each phrase. Begin each sentence with *I am/was. . . .* (Use *so* in all three sentences.)
   a. being born in (your country)

   Example: I was born in Russia, so I speak Russian.

   b. being the oldest/youngest/middle/only child in your family
   c. being a lazy/hard-working student

5. Write a sentence that tells two different careers you might have in the future. (Use *or*.)

Try It Out!   Choose one of the following and write a paragraph. In your paragraph, focus on writing compound sentences. Try to use the coordinating conjunctions *and*, *but*, *so*, and *or* at least one time each.

- Retell a short folktale from your culture.
- Retell a children's story that you know.
- Retell the plot of a movie that you have seen recently.

Punctuation

Three Comma Rules   Let's review two comma rules that you have learned and learn one new one.

Rule	Example
1. Put a comma after a time order signal that comes before the subject at the beginning of a sentence. *Then*, *soon*, and *now* are usually not followed by a comma.	Yesterday, I did homework for three hours. Finally, I was too tired to think. At 8:00, I fell asleep on the sofa. BUT Soon I started snoring.
2. Put a comma after the first sentence in a compound sentence. Put the comma before the coordinating conjunction. (Don't use a comma between two parts of a simple sentence.)	I was too tired to think, so I decided to take a break and watch TV for a while. BUT I woke up and finished my homework.
3. Put a comma between the items in a series of three or more items. The items may be words, phrases, or clauses. (Don't use a comma between only two items.)	I got up, took a shower, drank a cup of coffee, grabbed my books, and ran out the door. Red, white, and blue are the colors of the U.S. flag. BUT Red and gold are the school colors.

PRACTICE 3

Commas

A. In the following sentences, add commas wherever they are necessary.

1. Daisy Tomiko Keiko and Nina live near the college that they all attend.

2. Tomiko and Keiko are from Japan and Nina and Daisy are from Mexico.

3. Nina and Keiko have the same birthday. Both girls were born on June 3, on different continents.

4. Last week the girls decided to have a joint birthday party so, they invited several friends for dinner.

5. Nina wanted to cook Mexican food, but Keiko wanted to have Japanese food.

6. Finally they agreed on the menu.

7. They served Japanese *tempura* Mexican *arroz con pollo* Chinese stir-fried vegetables and American ice cream.

8. First Nina made the rice.

9. Then, Keiko cooked the *tempura*.

10. After that Tomiko prepared the vegetables.

11. After dinner Daisy served the dessert.

12. The guests could choose chocolate ice cream or vanilla ice cream with chocolate sauce.

B. Answer each question with a complete sentence.

1. When and where were you born? (Begin your answer with *I was born on . . . .*)

   _____

2. Where do you live now?

   _____

3. Name three of your favorite foods.

   _____

4. What do you usually do on weekends? (Name at least four activities.)

   _____

5. Name one thing that you always do and one thing that you never do on weekends.

   _____

6. What are two or three goals in your life? (Begin your answer with *I would like to . . . .*)

   _____

7. What do you do in the evening? (Begin your answer with *In the evening . . . .*)

   _____

The Writing Process

Freewriting

You remember that prewriting is the step in the writing process in which you get ideas. In Chapter 1, you learned about the prewriting technique called *listing*. Another prewriting technique is **freewriting**. When you freewrite, you write "freely"—without stopping—on a topic for a specific amount of time. You just write down sentences as you think of them without worrying about whether your sentences are correct or not. You also don't have to punctuate sentences or capitalize words. You can even write incomplete sentences or phrases. The main goal in freewriting is to keep your pencil moving across the paper.

Look at this example of freewriting on the topic "A Memorable Event in My Life."

MODEL
Freewriting

A Memorable Event in My Life

I'm supposed to freewrite for ten minutes about a memorable event in my life. I don't know what to write about. Maybe about my brother's boat accident. We were so scared. We thought he was going to drown. He was trapped under an overturned boat and didn't have any air to breathe. But it ended all right.

> He was rescued and had only a broken arm. What else can I write about? Oh!
> I know. A day I will always remember was the day I left my country to come to
> the United States. That was a sad/happy day. I felt sad and happy at the same
> time. Maybe I should write about something happy. Our family vacation last
> summer was fun. We drove to the coast and camped for a week on the beach.
> Then there was the day the earthquake happened. Now <u>that</u> was definitely
> a memorable event. I will never forget it. I was at home with my older sister
> and little brother. . . .

This writer freewrote until she found a good topic: the earthquake. If she had wanted to, she could have done further freewriting about her earthquake experience to develop this topic.

Try It Out!

Freewrite about a memorable event or experience in your life. It might be a happy day, a sad event, an embarrassing moment, an interesting trip, or a frightening experience. Write for about ten minutes without stopping. If you find a topic during your freewriting, continue freewriting on that topic. If you already have a topic in mind before you start, freewrite on that topic for ten minutes to develop your ideas about it.

Review

These are the important points covered in this chapter:

1. Narration is the kind of writing that you do when you tell a story.

2. Use time order words and phrases to show when each part of the story happens.

3. A compound sentence is composed of two simple sentences joined by a comma and a coordinating conjunction.

4. Four coordinating conjunctions are *and*, *but*, *so*, and *or*.

5. Commas are used

   - after most time order signals at the beginning of a sentence.
   - in compound sentences.
   - between items in a series.
   - in dates written in the order month-day-year.
   - in place names.

6. Freewriting is a prewriting technique in which you write without stopping for a specific amount of time.

Writing Assignment

Write a paragraph about a memorable event or a memorable experience in your life. Let's review the steps in the writing process.

Step 1 Prewrite to get ideas. Use the freewriting that you completed in the Try It Out! exercise.

Step 2 Organize the ideas. Put the events into time order: Make a list of the events or number them on your freewriting paper. Use your list to guide you as you write.

Step 3 Write the rough draft. Write ROUGH DRAFT at the top of your paper.

- Begin your paragraph with a sentence that tells what event or experience you are going to write about.

  I'll never forget the day I met my future husband.

  The most memorable vacation I ever took was a bicycle trip across Canada.

- Use time order to organize your paragraph. Use time order signals, and punctuate them correctly.
- Pay attention to your sentence structure. Write both simple and compound sentences, and punctuate them correctly.

Step 4 Polish the rough draft.

- Exchange papers with a classmate and ask him or her to check your rough draft using Peer-Editing Worksheet 2 on page 200. Then discuss the completed worksheet and decide what changes you should make. Write a second draft.
- Use Self-Editing Worksheet 2 on page 201 to check your second draft for grammar, punctuation, and sentence structure.

Step 5 Write a final copy. Hand in your rough draft, your second draft, your final copy, and the page containing the two editing worksheets. Your teacher may also ask you to hand in your prewriting paper.

Alternative Writing Assignment

Write a paragraph in which you explain how you celebrate a special day or special occasion in your culture. For example, a person living in the United States might write about Halloween, Thanksgiving Day, or St. Patrick's Day. Follow the writing process steps.

Paragraph Structure

Organization

As you learned in Chapter 1, a **paragraph** is a group of related sentences that develops one main idea, which is the topic of the paragraph. In this chapter you will study paragraph structure in detail.

Three Parts of a Paragraph

A paragraph has three parts: a **topic sentence**, several **supporting sentences**, and a **concluding sentence**.

1. The topic sentence tells what topic the paragraph is going to discuss.
2. The supporting sentences give details about the topic.
3. The concluding sentence summarizes the main points or restates the topic sentence in different words.

A paragraph is like a sandwich. The topic sentence and concluding sentences are the two pieces of "bread" enclosing the "meat"—the supporting sentences. A diagram of a paragraph looks like this:

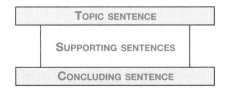

The model paragraph that follows describes a typical wedding in Hawaii. The people who live in the island state of Hawaii are from many different ethnic groups. In Hawaii, Hawaiians, Japanese, Chinese, Filipinos, Portuguese, and *haoles*[1] share their customs freely with one another. As you read the model, notice the three parts of the paragraph.

MODEL

Three Parts of a Paragraph

[1]TOPIC SENTENCE

[2-11]SUPPORTING SENTENCES

A Hawaiian Wedding

[1]The mix of cultures in Hawaii makes weddings there very special occasions. [2]Certainly, Hawaiian clothing, music, and other Hawaiian customs play a big role. [3]For example, the bride often wears a long white *holoku* (wedding dress), and the groom wears a long-sleeved white shirt and pants with a red sash around his waist. [4]Both the bride and the groom wear *leis*.[2] [5]The bride's *lei* is traditionally made of white flowers such as *pikake* (jasmine), and the groom's is made of

---

[1]*haoles:* Hawaiian word for people with white skin
[2]*leis:* necklaces made of flowers

green *maile* leaves. [6]Another Hawaiian custom is the blowing of a conch shell[3] three times to begin the ceremony. [7]Hawaiian music is played both during the ceremony and during the *luau*[4] afterward. [8]Other customs included in the festivities depend on the ethnic backgrounds of the couple. [9]For instance, there may be noisy firecrackers, a Chinese way of keeping bad spirits away. [10]There may be a display of Japanese *origami,*[5] or there may be a *pandango,* a Filipino custom. [11]During a *pandango,* the wedding guests tape money together and wrap it around the couple during their first dance together as husband and wife.

[12]CONCLUDING SENTENCE [12]All in all, a Hawaiian wedding is truly a magical, multicultural event.

Questions on the Model
1. Look at the title. What is the topic of the paragraph?
2. Look at the first sentence. What does it say about the topic?
3. Now look at the last sentence. What idea from the first sentence is repeated here?

Now let's study each of the three parts of a paragraph in more detail.

The Topic Sentence

The topic sentence is the most important sentence in a paragraph. It has two parts: a **topic** and a **controlling idea.** The topic names the subject of the paragraph. In our model, the topic is Hawaiian weddings. The controlling idea tells what the paragraph will say about the topic. It is called the *controlling idea* because it controls or limits the topic to a very specific point or points. In our model, the controlling idea is that weddings in Hawaii are special because of the mix of cultures.

Here are examples of topic sentences with the same topic but different controlling ideas:

TOPIC   CONTROLLING IDEA
1a. Some marriages are a union of two families.

TOPIC   CONTROLLING IDEA
1b. Some marriages are a union of two individuals.

TOPIC   CONTROLLING IDEA
2a. Some weddings are very elaborate.

TOPIC   CONTROLLING IDEA
2b. Some weddings are very simple.

TOPIC   CONTROLLING IDEA
2c. Some weddings take place in unusual locations.

----

[3]**conch shell:** large seashell that makes noise like a horn. In ancient Hawaii, blowing a conch shell marked the start of any important ceremony.
[4]*luau:* Hawaiian barbecue feast
[5]*origami:* Japanese art of folding paper into shapes

<table>
<tr>
<td>

PRACTICE 1

*Predicting
Content from the
Controlling Idea*

</td>
<td>

With a partner, a small group, or the whole class, talk about what information the paragraph for each of the following topic sentences might contain.

1. Some weddings are very elaborate.
2. Some weddings are very simple.
3. Some weddings take place in unusual locations.

</td>
</tr>
</table>

Position of the Topic Sentence   The topic sentence is usually the first sentence in a paragraph. Experienced writers sometimes put topic sentences at the end, but the best place is usually right at the beginning. A topic sentence at the beginning of a paragraph gives readers an idea of what they will read. This helps them understand the paragraph more easily.

Not Too General, Not Too Specific   A topic sentence is neither too general nor too specific.

TOO GENERAL   Marriage is an event in a person's life.

This is too general because there is no specific controlling idea. The reader has no idea what the paragraph will say about marriage except that it happens.

TOO SPECIFIC   The average age for people in the United States to marry in the year 2000 was 25 for a woman and 27 for a man.

This is much too specific. It gives details that should come later in the paragraph.

GOOD   The average age for people in the United States to marry has changed in the past 100 years.

This is a good topic sentence because it gives the reader a hint that the paragraph will discuss changes in the ages when people marry. A good topic sentence tells something about the contents of the paragraph but none of the details.

<table>
<tr>
<td>

PRACTICE 2

Topic Sentences

</td>
<td>

Work with a partner or in a small group.

A. Put a check (✓) next to good topic sentences. Tell what is wrong with the unchecked sentences. Are they too specific or too general? Write *Too specific* or *Too general* on the line.

</td>
</tr>
</table>

<u>Too specific</u>	1. It is estimated that 20 percent of Japanese marriages are arranged.
<u> ✓ </u>	2. In Japan, there are two types of marriage.
<u> </u>	3. Digital cameras have several advantages over film cameras.
<u> </u>	4. Digital cameras take photos.
<u> </u>	5. Digital photos are composed of small squares, just like a tiled kitchen floor or bathroom wall.
<u> </u>	6. Learning the meanings of abbreviations used in the field of technology is like learning a new language.

_____ 7. PC, PDA, GPS, and Wifi are abbreviations.

_____ 8. A PDA can perform a variety of useful functions.

_____ 9. Consider these four factors when choosing a college.

_____ 10. Golden retriever dogs have certain characteristics that make them good family pets.

_____ 11. I am considering event planning as a career.

_____ 12. A paramedic should have three characteristics.

B. Read the following paragraphs. Then choose the best topic sentence for each one from the list. Write that sentence on the line.

1. _____

_____. Trail climbing is the easiest. Climbers just walk along trails to the top of a mountain. The trails are not very steep, and the mountains are small. The second type, rock climbing, takes place on steeper slopes and bigger mountains. Climbers generally have to use special equipment such as climbing shoes, ropes, and metal nails called pitons. The third type is ice climbing. Ice climbing takes place only on very high mountains and requires a lot of special equipment. Equipment used in ice climbing includes ice axes and crampons, which are spikes attached to a climber's boots for walking on ice and hard snow. Indeed, the sport of mountain climbing can range from an easy uphill walk to a difficult climb up a frozen waterfall.

a. Mountain climbing requires special skills and equipment.
b. The sport of mountain climbing is practiced worldwide.
c. There are three main types of mountain climbing.

2. _____

_____. For example, Kansas City, in the very center of the United States, is known for its beef, and Kansas City barbecue is everyone's favorite way to enjoy it. In Boston, people love baked beans. In the Southwest, chili, a stew made of meat, beans, tomatoes, and hot peppers, is the regional dish. Wisconsin, a state with many dairy farms, is famous for its cheese. Go to Maryland and Virginia for crab cakes[1] and to the Northeast for clam chowder[2] and maple syrup.[3] Indeed, many U.S. cities and regions have a special food for everyone to enjoy.

a. There is a variety of food in the United States.
b. Food in the United States varies from sweet desserts to spicy stews.
c. Different regions of the United States have their own traditional foods.
d. Food in the United States is quite delicious.

(continued on next page)

---

[1]**crab cakes:** fried patties of crab, breadcrumbs, onions, and spices
[2]**chowder:** soup
[3]**maple syrup:** sweet sap (liquid) from maple trees boiled down to thicken it (similar to honey)

3. _____

_____. Before the 2004 tsunami in the
Indian Ocean, water buffalo stampeded[1] in Thailand, and dogs in Sri Lanka
refused to go out for their regular walks. An unusual number of pets
ran away from their homes in the days before the 1989 San Francisco
earthquake. Japanese researchers have analyzed fishermen's stories about
the abnormal behavior of fish in the days or hours before earthquakes in
that country. These are just a few examples of strange animal behavior
just before earthquakes occur.

a. Dogs, elephants, water buffalo, and fish can predict earthquakes.
b. Earthquake prediction is an important science.
c. Animals may be able to sense earthquakes before they happen.

C. Work with a partner, with a small group, or by yourself. Read each paragraph
and determine the topic and the controlling idea. Then write an appropriate
topic sentence on the line.

1. _____

_____. First of all, teachers must know
their subjects very well. At a minimum, they should take several college
courses and pass a written test in every subject that they teach. Also, they
should take refresher classes[2] every few years to keep their knowledge
up-to-date. Third, teachers should take education classes in college to learn
how to teach. Fourth, they should have spent at least one year practice-
teaching. Practice-teaching is teaching real children in a real classroom
under the supervision of an experienced teacher. Only after a person has
met these requirements should he or she receive a teaching license.

2. _____

_____. Even small towns in the United
States have at least one pizzeria and one Chinese restaurant. Every midsize
town has at least one taqueria, where you can get a delicious Mexican
taco or burrito. French food has always been popular, and hot dogs and
hamburgers, German in origin, are found everywhere. More recently, Middle
Eastern shish kebab, Japanese sushi, and English fish and chips are
increasingly available in the United States.

3. _____

_____. Some people skip breakfast because
they think it will help them lose weight. Another reason people give is that
they simply don't like breakfast. For others, the reason is cultural. People
in some cultures consume only two meals each day instead of three, and
breakfast isn't traditionally one of them. The most common reason people
give is lack of time. They like to stay in bed until the last minute, and then
they have to rush to get to work or to school on time.

---

[1]**stampeded:** ran away in panic
[2]**refresher classes:** classes that teach about new developments in a field

Developing Topic Sentences Imagine that you are given the topic *friends* to write a paragraph about. *Friends* is too large a topic for a paragraph, so you need to narrow it to a smaller topic. One way to do this is to use the listing technique that you learned in Chapter 1. Make a list of every word or phrase that comes into your mind about the word *friends*. Your list might look like this:

Friends

kinds of friends	friends from school
new friends	casual friends
old friends	how to make friends
best friend	what is a friend
childhood friends	

Then choose one of the smaller topics (one of the items from your list). You might choose "What is a friend?" Make a second list while thinking about this smaller topic.

What Is a Friend?

have fun with	is loyal
hang out with	can depend on
play sports with	ask advice
share secrets	help each other
can trust	enjoy the same activities
share problems	like the same movies, sports

Any of these ideas can be the controlling idea in your topic sentence:

A friend is a person you have fun with.
A friend is someone you can trust.
A friend is a person who enjoys the same activities.

Try It Out!   Work with a partner or with a small group. Use the listing technique and write a topic sentence on five of the following topics:

ways to meet people in a new place	disadvantages of growing up in a small town
kinds of video games/television programs/movies you enjoy	ways to waste time
advantages of being bilingual	foreign travel
advantages of growing up in a small town	

Supporting Sentences

Supporting sentences explain the topic by giving more information about it. **Supporting point sentences** list the main points of the paragraph.

> Certainly, Hawaiian clothing, music, and other Hawaiian customs play a big role.
>
> Other customs included in the festivities depend on the ethnic backgrounds of the couple.
>
> Some people skip breakfast because they think it will help them lose weight.
>
> Third, they should have spent at least one year practice-teaching.

PRACTICE 3

Writing Supporting Sentences

Work with a partner or in a small group. Read each topic sentence. Then fill in the blanks with additional supporting sentences. Add as many supporting sentences as you can, but you do not have to fill in all of the blanks.

1. Owning a small car has several advantages.

   a. A small car is easier to park. _____

   b. _____

   c. _____

   d. _____

2. To keep your teeth healthy and your smile bright, do the following things.

   a. Don't eat sugary foods. _____

   b. _____

   c. _____

   d. _____

3. Consider these three/four/five factors when planning a family vacation.

   a. Consider the interests of everyone. _____

   b. _____

   c. _____

   d. _____

4. A good friend has two/three/four important qualities.

   a. He/She can keep secrets. _____

   b. _____

   c. _____

   d. _____

5. Avoid studying for a big test by taking the following actions.

   a. Turn on the television, the radio, or your CD player. _____

   b. _____

   c. _____

6. A college education is important for these reasons.

    a. <u>It prepares you for a career.</u>

    b. _____

    c. _____

Examples

Examples illustrate the supporting point sentences. Examples are good support because they are specific; they make your meaning very clear.

Notice the **signal phrases** that can introduce examples. At the beginning of a sentence, use *For example* or *For instance*, followed by a comma. In front of an example that is just a word or phrase (not an entire sentence), use the prepositional phrase *such as* without a comma.[1]

Signal Phrases for Examples

Followed by a Comma	No Comma
1. For example, For instance,	2. such as

1. **For example,** the bride often wears a long white *holoku* (wedding dress), and the groom wears a long-sleeved white shirt and pants with a red sash around his waist.

   For instance, there may be noisy firecrackers, a Chinese way of keeping bad spirits away.

2. The bride's *lei* is traditionally made of white flowers **such as** *pikake* (jasmine), and the groom's is made of green *maile* leaves.

PRACTICE 4

Signal Phrases for Examples

Fill in each blank with one of these signal phrases: *For example*, *For instance*, or *such as*. Add commas where necessary. Use each phrase once.

    The city of London has many great tourist attractions. (1) _____ most tourists make a stop at Westminster Abbey. In this famous church, tourists can see where English kings and queens are crowned. Westminster Abbey is the burial place of famous people (2) _____ poet Geoffrey Chaucer, scientists Isaac Newton and Charles Darwin, and actor Laurence Olivier. Tourists also like to catch a glimpse of royal life while in London. (3) _____ they can watch the changing of the guard at Buckingham Palace, or they can tour the Tower of London, where the British crown jewels are kept.

---

[1]*Such as* is sometimes used with a comma.

PRACTICE 5

Supporting Sentences and Examples

Turn back to the model paragraph "A Hawaiian Wedding" on page 38 and complete the diagram. Copy the supporting sentences into the appropriate boxes. Notice that the paragraph has two supporting point sentences and several example sentences.

TOPIC SENTENCE

The mix of cultures in Hawaii makes weddings there very special occasions.

SUPPORTING POINT SENTENCE

Certainly, Hawaiian clothing, music, and other Hawaiian customs play a big role.

EXAMPLE

For example, the bride often wears a long white *holoku,* and the groom wears a long-sleeved white shirt and pants with a red sash around his waist.

EXAMPLE

Both the bride and the groom wear *leis*.

EXAMPLE

EXAMPLE

EXAMPLE

SUPPORTING POINT SENTENCE

EXAMPLE

EXAMPLE

EXAMPLE

During a *pandango,* the wedding guests tape money together and wrap it around the couple during their first dance together as husband and wife.

CONCLUDING SENTENCE

All in all, a Hawaiian wedding is truly a magical, multicultural event.

The Concluding Sentence

A concluding sentence signals the end of the paragraph and reminds the reader of the main idea.[1] Here are three tips to help you write a good concluding sentence:

1. Begin with a conclusion signal. Most conclusion signals have commas after them; others do not.

Conclusion Signals

Followed by a Comma		No Comma
1. All in all, In brief, In conclusion, Indeed, In short,	In summary, To conclude, To summarize, To sum up,	2. It is clear that . . . These examples show that . . . You can see that . . .

1. **To summarize,** Japanese food is both beautiful to look at and delicious to eat.

   Indeed, many U.S. cities and regions have a special food for everyone to enjoy.

2. **It is clear that** fad diets don't work and may even damage a dieter's health.

2. Remind your reader of the main idea by one of the following methods.

   • Repeat the idea in the topic sentence in different words. Do not just copy the topic sentence.

TOPIC SENTENCE

Successful bidding on eBay requires patience and strategy.

CONCLUDING SENTENCE

In conclusion, wait patiently and place your bid with precision timing, and you will be the winning bidder every time.

   • Summarize the main point or points of the paragraph.

CONCLUDING SENTENCE

In conclusion, follow the steps I have outlined, and you will be the winning bidder every time.

3. NEVER end a paragraph by introducing a new idea!

   X In conclusion, you can spend a lot of money on eBay.

PRACTICE 6

Concluding Sentences

Work with a partner or in a small group.

A. From the choices listed, choose the best concluding sentence for this paragraph. Be prepared to explain your choice to the class.

---

[1]Not all paragraphs need a concluding sentence. A paragraph that stands alone needs a concluding sentence, but a paragraph that is part of a longer piece of writing doesn't always need one.

Animals in Captivity

Animals living in modern zoos enjoy several advantages over animals in the wild. The first advantage is that zoo animals are separated from their natural predators.[1] They are protected, so they live without risk of being attacked. Another advantage is that someone feeds them regularly, so they do not have to hunt for food. Also, they do not suffer times when food is hard to find. A third advantage of living in zoos is that veterinarians give animals regular checkups, and sick animals get prompt medical attention.

_____

_____

1. In conclusion, because all their needs are taken care of, most zoo animals are healthy and contented.
2. In conclusion, living in a zoo has many advantages for animals, but it also has some disadvantages.
3. In conclusion, zoos keep animals safe from predators.

B. On the line at the end of each paragraph, write a concluding sentence. Be sure to begin with a conclusion signal.

1.　The college cafeteria is an inexpensive place to eat. For example, you can get a cheeseburger, french fries, and a soda for only $3.00. A slice of pizza is only $1.50, and a cup of coffee is only 50¢. There is a daily special for about $2.50. It includes an entrée, rice or potatoes, and a vegetable. The salad bar is the best deal of all. You get all you can eat for $2.00. _____

_____

2.　Watching children's programs on television is a good way to learn a foreign language. First, the actors speak slowly and repeat often. Also, the vocabulary is not difficult. Finally, there is always a lot of action, so you know what is happening even if you don't understand the words. _____

_____

---

[1]**predators:** animals that kill and eat other animals

3.   Cell phones have taken over! Any time of the day or night, you see automobile drivers chatting away at 65 miles per hour (mph) on the highway. On sidewalks, in restaurants, and even in office building elevators, cell phone users carry on the most private conversations. Many places of business now have signs asking people to turn off their cell phones, and phones are banned[2] in hospital waiting rooms, movie theaters, and concert halls. _____

PRACTICE 7

Paragraph Structure

The following sentences are a scrambled paragraph. Put the sentences in order and copy them in the diagram on page 50. This is how to proceed.

Step 1 Find the topic sentence. Give it the number 1.

Step 2 Find the concluding sentence. Give it the number 9.

Step 3 Then decide which sentences are supporting points and put them in order. Look for the words *First*, *Second*, *Third*, and *Finally*.

Step 4 Decide which examples support which points.

Step 5 Copy the sentences into the appropriate boxes.

Fast Food, Unhealthy Food[2]

_____ a. For example, a 6-inch Pizza Hut Personal Pan pepperoni pizza has 660 calories, and a McDonald's Big Mac has 560 calories.[3]

_____ b. In conclusion, a quick meal at a fast-food restaurant may be delicious and convenient, but it is definitely not a healthy way to eat.

_____ c. Second, a lot of the calories from fast food are from fat.

_____ d. Third, fast-food items such as hamburgers and french fries contain high amounts of salt.

_____ e. Fast food is extremely popular in the United States, but it is not very good for you.

_____ f. First of all, most fast food is very high in calories.

_____ g. A typical meal at McDonald's contains as much as 1,370 milligrams of sodium.[4]

_____ h. Finally, add a sugary soft drink to your fast-food meal, and you pound the last nail into the heart of any nutritionist.[5]

_____ i. For instance, a portion of Nachos Supreme from Taco Bell contains 26 grams of fat, and a Big Mac contains 30 grams.

---

[2]**banned:** not permitted

[3]McDonald's nutritional information obtained on Jan. 29, 2006 from http://www.mcdonalds.com/app_controller.nutrition.index1.html. Pizza Hut nutritional information obtained on Jan. 29, 2006 from <http://www.yum com/nutrition/results.asp?BrandID=1&BrandAbbr=PH>. Taco Bell nutritional information obtained on Jan. 29, 2006 from http://www.yum.com/nutrition/results.asp?BrandID=5&BrandAbbr=TB.

[4]**sodium:** salt

[5]**nutritionist:** person who studies healthful eating

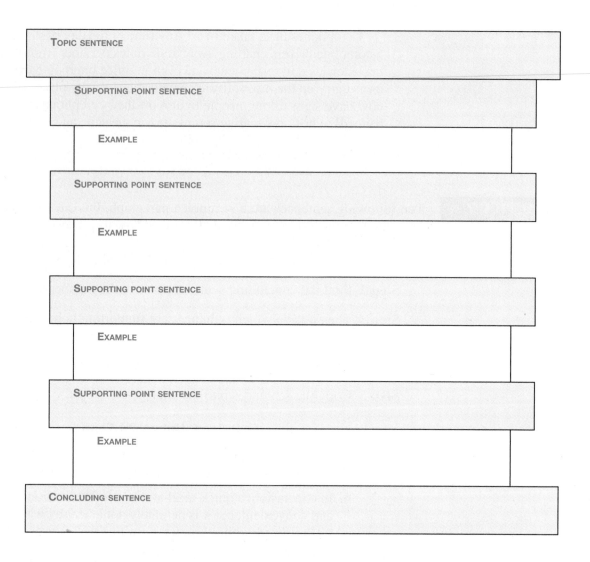

Try It Out!   Choose one of the topic sentences that you wrote in the Try It Out! exercise on page 43. Then use either listing or freewriting to get ideas for supporting sentences. On a separate piece of paper, make a diagram of boxes like the one above and fill it in. Be sure to add a concluding sentence.

Punctuation

Apostrophes   The apostrophe mark (') has three main uses in English:

- To make contractions
- To make nouns and some pronouns possessive
- To make letters of the alphabet plural

Contractions

An apostrophe shows where letters are missing in a contraction.

isn't	is not	won't	will not
she's	she is OR she has	they're	they are
it's	it is	they'd	they had OR they would

We use contractions in conversation and in informal writing such as letters to friends, but we usually do not use them in formal academic and business writing. (Some teachers allow contractions; others do not. Ask your teacher.)

Possessives

Possessive words show ownership. In the phrase *Maria's book, Maria's* is a possessive noun showing that Maria is the owner of the book.

In English, we can show ownership with nouns in two ways. We can use an *of the* phrase and say *the name of my friend*, or we can use an apostrophe + *s* and say *my friend's name*.

the speed of the runner	OR	the runner's speed
the orders of the doctor	OR	the doctor's orders
the complaints of my neighbor	OR	my neighbor's complaints

- In general, we use an apostrophe or an apostrophe + *s* more often when the owner is a living being, and we use the *of* phrase more often when the owner is a nonliving thing. We prefer, for example, to say *the dog's leg* but *the leg of the table*. Sometimes you can write a possessive either way: *The bank's president* or *the president of the bank*.

- When the owner's name is given, we don't have a choice. We must use an apostrophe or apostrophe + *s*.

Maria's book	NOT	the book of Maria
the Smiths' house	NOT	the house of the Smiths

- Besides nouns, we also make indefinite pronouns possessive. Indefinite pronouns are the words *someone, anyone, somebody, anybody, everyone, everybody, no one, nobody,* and *one.*

someone's jacket
anybody's mistake

Follow these rules to make nouns and indefinite pronouns possessive.

Rules for Forming Possessives

Add an Apostrophe + *s*		
Rule	**Singular Nouns**	**Plural Nouns**
1. to singular nouns and to plural nouns that don't end in *s*.	child**'s** toy boss**'s** office Mr. and Mrs. Smith**'s** house Mr. and Mrs. Jones**'s** children	children**'s** game men**'s** shirts women**'s** dresses
2. to indefinite pronouns.	someone**'s** jacket nobody**'s** fault	
3. to abbreviations.	NAFTA**'s** success the UN**'s** members	
Add an Apostrophe Alone		
to plural nouns ending in *s*.		engineering students**'** club actresses**'** performances the Smiths**'** house the Joneses**'** children

Plural of Letters of the Alphabet

Use an apostrophe + *s* to make letters of the alphabet plural.

> There are four *s***'s** and four *i***'s** in the word *Mississippi*.
> The teacher gave ten A**'s** and two F**'s** last semester.

Caution!

1. Don't confuse *it's* and *its*. *It's* is a contraction of *it is*. *Its* is a possessive pronoun. Possessive pronouns (*my*, *your*, *our*, *his*, *her*, *its*, *their*) never have apostrophes.

   > **It's** hot today.   The book lost **its** cover.

2. Don't confuse the contraction of a noun + *is* and the possessive form of the noun.

   > **John's** sick today. *(John is sick today.)*
   > **John's** car is a Toyota. *(The car that belongs to John is a Toyota.)*

3. Don't use an apostrophe to make nouns plural.

   > It is the policy of many companies to hire student interns during the summer.
   > The Smiths have a new baby daughter.

PRACTICE 8

Apostrophes

A. Change each item into a possessive phrase containing an apostrophe or an apostrophe + *s*.

1. the roommate of Joanna   _____ Joanna's roommate _____

2. the roommate of Carlos   _____

3. the flag of my country   _____

4. the feet of the dancers   _____

5. the school of my child   _____

6. the school of my children   _____

7. the secretary of the boss   _____

8. the shoes of ladies   _____

9. the sweaters of men   _____

10. the films of George Lucas   _____

11. the president of the EU   _____

B. Make a possessive phrase from the two parts of each item. Use an *of the* phrase, an apostrophe, or an apostrophe + *s*.

1. the heart + problem   _____ the heart of the problem _____

2. the heart + Lance Armstrong   _____

3. the color + her dress   _____

4. the desk + teacher   _____

5. the laughter + children   _____

6. the mouths + babies   _____

7. the mouth + river   _____

8. the suitcases + passengers   _____

C. Write eight sentences, using a possessive phrase in each. You may use a possessive phrase from Parts A and B of this practice, or you may use possessive phrases of your own invention.

1. I haven't met Carla's roommate yet. _____

2. The psychologist immediately understood the heart of the problem. _____

3. _____

4. _____

5. _____

6. _____

7. _____

(continued on next page)

8. _____

9. _____

10. _____

The Writing Process

Outlining   The best way to organize a paragraph is to make an outline before you begin to write. An outline is like an architect's plan for a house. Imagine building a house without a plan. The kitchen might be far away from the dining room, or the house might have no windows. Having a plan not only helps you, the writer, to organize your thoughts but it also ensures that you don't leave out anything important.

In Chapter 1, you practiced making simple outlines, which look like this:

Simple Outline

Topic sentence
    A. Supporting point
    B. Supporting point
    C. Supporting point
        (etc.)
Concluding sentence

When you filled in the boxes in the diagrams on pages 46 and 50, you were making outlines. Now learn a more formal way to do it.

A formal outline with details might look like this. Notice the system of letters and numbers. Also notice that each group of letters (A, B, C) and numbers (1, 2, 3) is indented.

Detailed Outline

Topic sentence
    A. Supporting point
        1. Detail (example, etc.)
        2. Detail
        3. Detail
    B. Supporting point
        1. Detail (example, etc.)
        2. Detail
        3. Detail
    C. Supporting point
        1. Detail (example, etc.)
        2. Detail
        3. Detail
Concluding sentence

MODEL

Detailed Outline

Music Styles and Fashion

Different styles of popular music have produced their own fashion styles.

    A. Punk fashion
       1. Spiked hair
       2. Theatrical makeup
       3. Safety-pin jewelry
       4. Ripped clothing
       5. Body piercing
    B. Hip-hop fashion
       1. Baggy jeans, worn low
       2. Hooded sweaters
       3. Big, floppy hats
       4. Do-rags (scarves) around head
    C. Grunge fashion
       1. Stonewashed jeans
       2. Plaid flannel shirts
       3. Baseball caps worn backward
       4. Long, straight hair
       5. Heavy boots

You can identify a person's musical taste by the clothes he or she wears.

In this detailed outline, supporting points A, B, and C support the topic sentence. Details 1 through 4 and 1 through 5 explain each supporting point. Of course, outlines are usually not as regular as these models. Every outline will probably have a different number of supporting points and a different number of details.

PRACTICE 9

Outlining

A. Complete the outline of the paragraph "Animals in Captivity" on page 48.

TOPIC SENTENCE

Animals living in modern zoos enjoy several advantages over animals in the wild.

    A. _____
       1. _____
    B. _____
       1. _____
    C. _____

CONCLUDING SENTENCE
_____

B. On a separate piece of paper, make an outline of the following paragraph:

Bad Drivers

¹There are three kinds of bad drivers you see on the streets and highways of almost any country. ²The first kind of bad driver is the wannabe¹ Grand Prix racer. ³This kind of driver drives very aggressively. ⁴For example, he or she steps on the gas and roars away a millisecond² before a traffic signal turns green. ⁵Driving in the passing lane and ignoring speed limits are normal for this kind of driver. ⁶The second kind of bad driver is the modern multitasker.³ ⁷Modern multitaskers include drivers such as working mothers and overworked businessmen and women. ⁸They eat a sandwich, drink a cup of coffee, talk on their cell phone, and discipline the children fighting in the back seat while speeding down the highway at 65 mph. ⁹The last kind is the cautious driver. ¹⁰The cautious driver drives v-e-r-y slowly and carefully. ¹¹For instance, he or she drives no faster than 40 mph on highways and slows down to 30 on every curve. ¹²When making a turn, he or she almost comes to a full stop before inching around the corner. ¹³In conclusion, bad drivers can be speedsters, "slowsters," or just inattentive, but you have to watch out for all of them!

Review

These are the important points covered in this chapter:

1. A paragraph has three parts: a topic sentence, several supporting sentences, and a concluding sentence.

   - The topic sentence is the most important sentence in a paragraph. It is usually the first sentence.
   - A good topic sentence has both a topic and a controlling idea. The controlling idea gives the reader a hint about what the paragraph will say about the topic.

2. Supporting sentences explain the controlling idea in detail.

3. The concluding sentence repeats the main idea in different words or summarizes the main supporting points. It usually begins with a conclusion signal.

---

¹**wannabe:** someone who wants to be something he or she is not (informal)
²**millisecond:** very short period of time, 1/1000 of a second
³**multitasker:** person who performs many tasks at the same time (informal)

4. Apostrophes are used in three ways:

- To form contractions
- To form possessives
- To make letters of the alphabet plural

5. A detailed outline is helpful for organizing ideas.

Writing Assignment

Choose one of the topic sentences from Practice 2 on page 40 and write a paragraph. Follow the steps in the writing process. You may use the topic you have worked on in the Try It Out! exercise on page 43, or you may use a different topic sentence.

Step 1 Prewrite to get ideas.

Step 2 Organize the ideas by making an outline.

Step 3 Write the rough draft. Write ROUGH DRAFT at the top of your paper. Focus on paragraph structure.

- Begin your paragraph with a clear topic sentence.
- Write several supporting sentences. Include some specific examples.
- End with a good concluding sentence.

Step 4 Polish the rough draft.

- Exchange papers with a classmate and ask him or her to check your rough draft using Peer-Editing Worksheet 3 on page 202. Then discuss the completed worksheet and decide what changes you should make. Write a second draft.
- Use Self-Editing Worksheet 3 on page 203 to check your second draft for grammar, punctuation, and sentence structure.

Step 5 Write a final copy. Hand in your rough draft, your second draft, your final copy, and the page containing the two editing worksheets. Your teacher may also ask you to hand in your prewriting paper.

Summary Writing 1

A **summary** is a short statement that gives the main information about something without giving all the details. The ability to summarize information is a useful writing skill. In your college classes, you will need to summarize information from your textbooks on tests. In some classes, you will also write original papers in which you summarize information from outside reading.

You already know how to summarize in speaking. You summarize every day. For example, when you retell a story that you have read or heard, you are summarizing. When you tell a friend the plot of a movie that you have seen, you are summarizing.

A summary, then, is a short retelling in your own words. In this section, you will learn how to do it in writing.

First, reread the model paragraph from page 38, "A Hawaiian Wedding." Then read the summary.

Original Paragraph

A Hawaiian Wedding

The mix of cultures in Hawaii makes weddings there very special occasions. Certainly, Hawaiian clothing, music, and other Hawaiian customs play a big role. For example, the bride often wears a long white *holoku* (wedding dress), and the groom wears a long-sleeved white shirt and pants with a red sash around his waist. Both the bride and the groom wear *leis*. The bride's *lei* is traditionally made of white flowers such as *pikake* (jasmine), and the groom's is made of green *maile* leaves. Another Hawaiian custom is the blowing of a conch shell three times to begin the ceremony. Hawaiian music is played both during the ceremony and during the *luau* afterward. Other customs included in the festivities depend on the ethnic backgrounds of the couple. For instance, there may be noisy firecrackers, a Chinese way of keeping bad spirits away. There may be a display of Japanese origami, or there may be a *pandango*, a Filipino custom. During a *pandango,* the wedding guests tape money together and wrap it around the couple during their first dance together as husband and wife. All in all, a Hawaiian wedding is truly a magical, multicultural event. (194 words)

Summary

Weddings in Hawaii combine customs from many cultures. Hawaiian customs may include the clothing worn by the couple, the flowers, the music, and the type of party after the ceremony. Chinese, Japanese, and Filipino customs may also play a part depending on the ethnicity[1] of the bride and groom. (49 words)

Notice that the summary gives the two main points—(1) Hawaiian customs and (2) customs of other ethnic groups—but no details. The summary does not describe the clothing, tell what kind of flowers, or talk about *pandango*, *origami*, or firecrackers.

As you can see, the summary (49 words) is much shorter than the original (194 words). When you write a summary, write the important ideas in as few words as possible.

There are three keys to writing a summary:

1. Include only main points; leave out details.
2. Use your own words. Do not copy sentences from the original.
3. Do not add any ideas that are not in the original.

---

[1]**ethnicity:** race or national group

EXERCISE

Summary Writing

A. You may work with a partner or with a small group of classmates on this exercise. Turn back to Chapter 1 page 5 and reread the model paragraph "Introducing Myself."

Imagine that you have a job as assistant personnel manager at a small medical clinic with Spanish-speaking patients. Marciela Perez has applied for a job as a receptionist there. Your job requires you to write a summary of every job applicant's background.

Step 1 What five pieces of information from "Introducing Myself" would be useful for your boss to know about Marciela? Write five questions asking for that information in the lines that follow. Write questions only about information that is relevant to the job. Also, consider only information that she has written. Do not add any ideas of your own.

1. _____

2. _____

3. _____

4. _____

5. _____

Step 2 Now write a short paragraph summarizing the five pieces of information. Use the memo form below. Write complete sentences, but use as few words as possible. Your summary should be about 40 to 50 words long.

MISSION STREET MEDICAL CLINIC
MEMO

DATE: _____

TO: <u>Personnel Manager</u>

FROM: _____
        (your name)

RE: <u>Marciela Perez</u>

_____

_____

_____

_____

_____

_____

_____

B. For additional practice, write a summary of the following paragraphs:

"A Person Who Has Made a Difference: George Lucas," page 10
"Bad Drivers," page 56

Descriptive Paragraphs

Organization

Descriptive writing appeals to the senses, so it tells how something looks, feels, smells, tastes, and/or sounds. A good description is a word picture; the reader can imagine the object, place, or person in his or her mind.

A description usually follows a pattern of organization that we call **spatial order**. Spatial order is the arrangement of things in space. As you read the model paragraph, notice how the description moves from the bottom of the stairway to the top. Also notice how the description of the woman moves from far away to near.

MODEL

Descriptive Paragraph

The Stairway[1]

[1]When I was two or three years old, I lived in a house that had a strange atmosphere. [2]I do not remember anything about the house except the stairway. [3]It was dark, squeaking, and quite narrow, and its steps were a little high for me to climb up. [4]From the bottom of the stairway, it seemed like an endless climb to the top. [5]Beyond the darkness at the top of the stairway, there was an elegant, middle-aged lady leaning against the wall. [6]I had to pass her every time I went to my room, for my room was the first room beyond the stairs on the second floor. [7]The lady wore a beautiful dress with a quiet pattern and a tinge[2] of blue, and her peaceful eyes stared at me every time I went up the stairs. [8]As I carefully climbed up the last step, her eyes became fixed[3] on me. [9]She didn't talk, nor did she move. [10]She just stood there and watched me clamber[4] up the stairs. [11]One day I touched her, but she did not react. [12]Her face did not change expression, nor did she even blink. [13]She just kept staring at me with her glittering[5] eyes. [14]Later, we moved out of the house, and I never saw her again. [15]Now I know that the lady was a mannequin.[6] [16]My aunt, who lived in the house, used it for her dressmaking class. [17]I did not know my mother. [18]Maybe I imagined that the mannequin standing at the top of the stairs was my mother. [19]The stairway with the strange atmosphere has an important place in my earliest memories.

(continued on next page)

---

[1]by student Toshiki Yamazaki
[2]**tinge:** small amount
[3]**fixed:** not moving
[4]**clamber:** climb with difficulty
[5]**glittering:** shining, sparkling
[6]**mannequin:** life-size model of a human used for displaying clothes

Questions on the Model
1. What does the writer say about the atmosphere of the house in the first sentence?
2. How does the writer describe the stairway? Underline the words that describe it.
3. When the writer first describes the woman, is he looking up at her or down at her? What does he describe about her first? What does he describe last?

Spatial Order

Just as an artist plans where to place each object in a painting, a writer plans where to put each object in a word picture. In a **description**, writers often use **spatial order** to organize their ideas. Spatial order is the arrangement of items in order by space.

For example, when describing your favorite room at home, you could first describe things on the left side of the doorway and then move clockwise around to the right side. You could also start on the right and move counterclockwise around to the left.

The model paragraph "The Stairway" uses spatial organization. In describing the stairway, the writer shows that as a little boy, his first view was from the bottom looking up at the mannequin. Then he climbs up the stairway. The spatial organization is from bottom to top. When he describes the mannequin, he first gives an overall impression (the way she was leaning against the wall and what her dress looked like). Then he focuses on her face and finally on her unblinking eyes. The spatial organization is from far to near.

It does not usually matter whether the spatial organization is left to right, right to left, near to far, far to near, outside to inside, inside to outside, top to bottom, or bottom to top. It is only helpful to use some kind of spatial order when you write a description.

Spatial Order Signals

Just as there are words and phrases to show time order, there are words and phrases to show spatial organization. They are often prepositional phrases of location or position. Notice the kinds of expressions used to show time order.

Spatial Order Signals	
at the top of	next to
in the center	between
on the left	behind
in front of	in back of
in the front of	in the back of
inside	across
_____	_____
_____	_____
_____	_____
_____	_____

PRACTICE 1

Spatial Order Signals

Find and underline the spatial order words and phrases used in the model paragraph "The Stairway" on page 61. Add them to the Spatial Order Signals chart.

Topic Sentences for Descriptive Paragraphs

The topic sentence of a descriptive paragraph should name the topic. The controlling idea should give the overall impression of the place you are describing. In the model paragraph, the topic is the house that the writer lived in as a child. The controlling idea is that it had a strange atmosphere. Each of the following sentences also states a topic and a controlling idea.

> My bedroom at home is my refuge from the outside world.
>
> The campus of our school is like a small city.
>
> The cafeteria at lunchtime is the school's social center.

PRACTICE 2

Spatial Order Organization and Details

A. Work with a classmate, a small group, or the whole class. Read the following topic sentences for descriptive paragraphs. Then discuss with your partner or group some possible details to describe the place. Next, decide on the best kind of spatial order to use in the description: right to left, left to right, top to bottom, far to near, outside to inside, and so on. Finally, write your details in spatial order on the lines.

1. After my sister spends two hours getting ready to go out, her room looks as if it had been hit by a magnitude 8.5 earthquake.

   a. From the doorway, you see nothing but a mountain of clothes all over the floor.

   b. _____

   _____

   c. _____

   _____

2. The park near my house is full of activity on a sunny weekend afternoon.

   a. _____

   _____

   b. _____

   _____

   c. _____

   _____

(continued on next page)

3. My uncle's workshop is a model of neatness and organization.

a. _____

_____

b. _____

_____

c. _____

_____

B. In the space below, draw a map of your neighborhood or a floor plan of your house, apartment, or bedroom. Then describe it to a classmate, using spatial order to organize your description and spatial order signals. If you like challenges, don't show the map/floor plan to your classmate, and see how accurately he or she can draw it from your description!

Try It Out!   Choose one of the items from Practice 2A or 2B and write a paragraph. Use spatial organization and spatial order signals to describe the place. If you choose to write your paragraph about 2B, be sure to begin with a topic sentence that gives a general impression.

Supporting Sentences for Descriptive Paragraphs

As you know, supporting sentences are the "meat" of a paragraph. They not only provide the details that prove the truth of your topic sentence, but they also make your writing rich and interesting. In a descriptive paragraph, the more details you include, the more clearly your reader will imagine what you are describing. Your details should appeal to the five senses. They should tell your reader how something looks, smells, sounds, feels, and tastes. Write about colors, sizes, shapes, odors, noises, and textures.

As you read the following model, underline the descriptive details that appeal to the senses. Look for colors, sounds, and textures.

MODEL

Descriptive Details

My Banana Garden[1]

[1]Behind my childhood home, there is a large piece of land that is surrounded by banana trees growing in wild disorder. [2]Crowds of banana trees grow freely everywhere. [3]Their green leaves are so thick that sunlight cannot pass through. [4]Underneath the trees, the ground is so moist that wild mushrooms and plants grow there all year around. [5]In the center is a wild field where the children of my village often fly kites. [6]Every evening, just before sunset, some birds arrive to look for a place to rest their tired wings. [7]They want to land in the dark banana garden, but the banana leaves are too wide to be made into nests. [8]The birds cry out and then fly away, seeking a better place to nest. [9]During the rainy season, it rains for days and days, and the banana leaves become glossy and slick. [10]The rain also makes the banana garden produce a very strange melody. [11]On rainy days, I used to sit near my window and listen to this wonderful song. [12]Now, whenever I hear the plop-plop-plop of raindrops on the roof of my small, tidy[2] apartment in the city, I remember the beautiful, wild banana garden of my childhood.

Questions on the Model
1. Find the topic sentence of this paragraph. What is the topic? The controlling idea?
2. Does the paragraph have a concluding sentence?
3. Circle any spatial order expressions you can find. Add them to the Spatial Order Signals chart on page 62. Is there a spatial order pattern or no pattern?
4. What adjective is repeated four times in the paragraph (in sentences 1, 4, 5, and 12)?

---

[1]by student Quang Nguyen
[2]**tidy:** neat, not messy

PRACTICE 3

*Descriptive
Details*

A. Reread the paragraph "My Banana Garden" and notice the supporting details. Which of the senses does the writer of this paragraph appeal to in his description: sight, smell, sound, touch, and/or taste? List the details in the paragraph that appeal to each sense. (There may not be any details for some of the senses.) In your opinion, do the details support the controlling idea, or not?

Sight	Smell	Sound	Touch	Taste
wild disorder				

B. Work with a classmate, a small group, or the whole class. Brainstorm together to think of descriptive details for the following topics. List as many sights, smells, sounds, etc., as you can.

1. A storm

   dark, cloudy, dark clouds, howling wind, wet sidewalk, slick streets _____

   _____

   _____

2. A subway station (or a bus stop) at rush hour

   _____

   _____

   _____

3. A busy airport terminal

   _____

   _____

   _____

4. The emergency room of a hospital

   _____

   _____

   _____

5. A sunny day at the beach

_____

_____

_____

Paragraph Unity

An important element of a good paragraph is **unity**. When a paragraph has unity, all the supporting sentences discuss only one idea. From beginning to end, each sentence is directly related to the topic. In some languages, it is acceptable to wander away from the topic—to make little side trips to ideas that are somewhat, but not directly, related to the main topic. In English, doing so is not acceptable because it breaks the unity of the paragraph.

Find and cross out sentences that are off the topic. Cross out two sentences in paragraph 1 and one sentence in paragraph 2.

1.

Havasu Canyon

¹There is a canyon in northern Arizona that is the most beautiful spot on Earth. ²It is called Havasu Canyon, and it is part of the Havasupai tribal reservation.¹ ³It is not easy to get there, for you have to hike down a long, hot trail. ⁴At the end of the trail is Supai Village. ⁵The Havasupai are a tribe of about 650 people. ⁶Their language has been written down only in the past twenty years. ⁷Beyond the village, another trail leads to the top of a steep cliff overlooking Havasu Canyon. ⁸Your first view of the canyon takes your breath away. ⁹Directly in front of you, the trail disappears straight down the 200-foot cliff. ¹⁰On your right, you see a beautiful waterfall. ¹¹Water pours straight down into a bright blue-green pool at the bottom of the canyon. ¹²Directly across the canyon, hundreds of small waterfalls gush from the cliff face, and little green ferns grow everywhere. ¹³At the bottom, the water cascades² from one turquoise pool into another until it disappears into the trees on the left. ¹⁴As you view this scene, you can only think that Havasu Canyon is truly a magical place.

_____

¹**reservation:** area of land where Native Americans live
²**cascades:** falls in steps

2.   **My First Apartment**

^1^My first apartment was very small. ^2^It was a studio apartment, so it had only one main room and a bathroom. ^3^The main room was divided into three areas. ^4^At one end of it was a kitchenette, where I cooked and ate my meals. ^5^My living/sleeping area was at the opposite end. ^6^I had just enough space for a bed, a coffee table, a floor lamp, and a small television. ^7^My study area was against the back wall. ^8^I lived there for two years, but I moved because my landlord raised the rent. ^9^My apartment was so small that I could never invite more than three friends at the same time!

Try It Out!   Write a paragraph describing one of the items in Practice 3B. Begin with a topic sentence that names what you will describe and gives a general impression of it:

The airport terminal is full of people in a hurry.

Focus on using lots of descriptive supporting details to make your word picture lively and interesting.

Sentence Structure

MODEL

Compound Sentences

Supai Village

^1^The trail to Supai Village is hot and dusty. ^2^You can hike the trail, or you can hire a guide to take you on horseback. ^3^Along the trail, you see only rock, sand, and an occasional lizard.[1] ^4^It is very dry, for this is desert country. ^5^There is no water on the trail, nor is there any shade. ^6^As you enter the village, you pass by several small homes. ^7^It is a quiet place. ^8^Dogs sleep in the streets, and villagers stand in their doorways and silently watch you, a stranger, pass by. ^9^They aren't smiling, yet they don't seem unfriendly. ^10^In the center of the village, there is a small hotel, a restaurant, a general store, and a post office. ^11^At the opposite end of the village, the trail leads to a cliff overlooking the canyon below.

Questions on the Model
1. In sentence 1, underline the subject(s) with one line and the verb(s) with two lines. Is this a simple or a compound sentence?
2. Do the same for sentences 2 and 3. What kind of sentences are they?

---

[1]**lizard:** reptile (kind of animal) that lives in dry areas

Compound Sentences with *yet, for,* and *nor*

You remember from Chapter 2 that a compound sentence is composed of two simple sentences joined by a comma and a coordinating conjunction. There are seven coordinating conjunctions in English. In that chapter, you practiced using *and, but, or,* and *so.* In this chapter, you will learn to use the other three: *yet, for,* and *nor.*

Coordinating Conjunctions

Coordinating Conjunction	Example
Yet has approximately the same meaning as *but*; that is, it shows contrast or joins opposites. Use *yet* when the second part of the sentence says something unexpected or surprising.	I was scared, **yet** I was also curious about the old lady. The weather is beautiful, **yet** it is supposed to rain today.
For has the same meaning as *because*; use *for* to introduce a reason or cause.	It is not easy to get there, **for** you have to hike down a long, hot trail.
Nor means "not this and not that"; use *nor* to join two negative sentences. *Note*: Use question word order after *nor*. Place helping verbs (*is, does, did, can, will,* etc.) before the subject.	She didn't talk, **nor** did she move. (She didn't talk. She didn't move.) The book isn't very long, **nor** is it difficult to read. (The book isn't long. It isn't difficult to read.)

PRACTICE 5

Compound Sentences with yet, for, *and* nor

A. Underline five compound sentences in the model paragraph on page 68. Circle the coordinating conjunctions.

B. Join the two sentences in each of the following pairs by using a comma and one of these coordinating conjunctions: *yet, for, nor.*

1. Muslims do not drink alcohol. They do not eat pork.

   _____

2. Some Christians do not work on Sunday. Sunday is their day to worship.

   _____

3. People who believe in the Hindu religion do not eat beef. They believe that cows are sacred.

   _____

4. Muslim men are permitted to have four wives. Few of them have more than one.

   _____

5. Buddhist monks do not marry. They do not own property.

   _____

C. Make compound sentences by adding another simple sentence that fits the meaning to each item.

1. I have studied English in school for six years, yet _____

_____ .

2. Many children who watch television all day long don't learn how to read well, for _____

_____ .

3. In some countries, women cannot vote, nor _____

_____ .

4. The United States is one of the richest countries in the world, yet _____

_____ .

5. Everyone should know at least two languages, for _____

_____ .

D. For additional practice, write one compound sentence of your own using *for*, *yet*, and *nor* one time each.

_____

_____

_____

Varying Sentence Openings

As you learned in Chapter 1, a prepositional phrase consists of a preposition and a pronoun, noun, or noun phrase. The following prepositional phrases express time, place, and possession, among other things.

Time	Place	Possession
in the early morning	in the hall	(the color) of the house
at 3:00	beyond the darkness	(the top) of the stairway
during dinner	in front of the house	(a girl) with red hair
after the accident	at the top of the stairs	

Some (but not all) prepositional phrases can come at the beginning as well as in the middle and at the end of a sentence. At the beginning of sentences, they often function as time order and spatial order signals. Moving prepositional phrases to the beginning of some sentences also adds interest and variety to your writing. When you use time order or spatial order in a paragraph, move some prepositional phrases to the beginning of their sentences, and put a comma after them.

I was afraid of many things during my childhood.
OR
During my childhood, I was afraid of many things.

You arrive at Havasupai Village at the end of the trail.
OR
At the end of the trail, you arrive at Havasupai village.

Not all prepositional phrases can be moved.

The color of the house was white.

NOT POSSIBLE   ~~Of the house, the color was white.~~

He married a girl with red hair.

NOT POSSIBLE   ~~With red hair, he married a girl.~~

PRACTICE 6

Varying Sentence Openings

Step 1 Underline all the prepositional phrases in the following sentences.

Step 2 When possible, rewrite sentences by moving a prepositional phrase to the beginning of its sentence.

Step 3 Punctuate your new sentences correctly.

1. A large earthquake occurred <u>under the Indian Ocean</u> <u>on December 26, 2004.</u>

   On December 26, 2004, a large earthquake occurred under the _____

   Indian Ocean. _____

2. The resulting tsunami[1] flooded the shores of several countries and killed nearly 250,000 people.

   _____

   _____

3. Hundred-foot waves crashed into homes and businesses in the towns near the coast.

   _____

   _____

4. The giant earthquake came just three days after a slightly smaller earthquake between Australia and New Zealand.

   _____

   _____

5. The energy released by the earthquake continued to be felt for several months after the event.

   _____

   _____

---

[1]**tsunami:** very large wave caused by an earthquake

The Writing Process

Clustering

In Chapter 1, you learned about the prewriting technique called *listing*. Now learn to use **clustering** as a way to get ideas for your writing.

When you cluster, you start by writing your topic in a circle in the middle of your paper. As you think of related ideas, you write these ideas in smaller circles around the first circle. The related idea in each small circle may produce even more ideas and therefore more circles around it. When you have run out of ideas, your paper might look something like the following model. The model paragraph "The Stairway" on page 61 was written from this model.

MODEL

Clustering

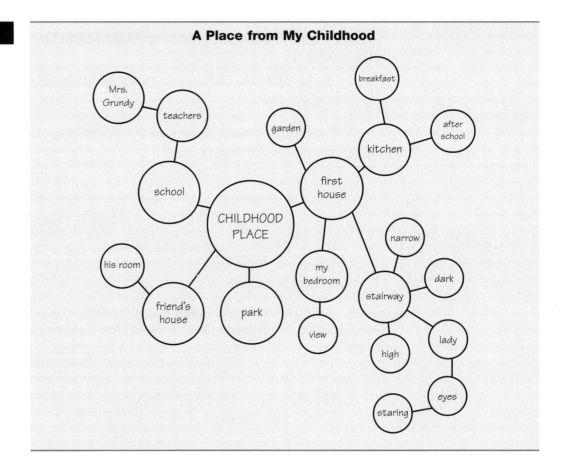

A Place from My Childhood

You can see that this writer had the most ideas about the first house he lived in as a child. When he thought more about his house, he remembered a stairway in the house and a mysterious lady at the top of it. Because of the richness of his ideas about the stairway, which you can see from the large number of circles, he chose it as the topic of his paragraph.

Try It Out!

Practice the clustering technique to develop a topic.

Step 1 Choose one of the topic suggestions, and write it in a large circle in the center of a piece of paper.

Step 2 Think about the topic for one or two minutes. Then write each new idea that comes into your mind in smaller circles around the large circle.

Step 3 Think about the idea in each smaller circle for one or two minutes. Write any new ideas in even smaller circles.

Step 4 Look over your groups of circles. Which group is the largest? The largest group of circles is probably the most productive topic for your paragraph.

Topic Suggestions
a place from my childhood
a place that is special to me
the view from my window
my favorite room
an unforgettable scene or view
a scene from a dream
my ideal room or apartment
my neighborhood

Review

These are the important points covered in this chapter:

1. A description is a word picture. It tells the reader how something looks, feels, smells, tastes, and sounds.

   - Use spatial order to organize a description. Spatial order is the arrangement of items in order by space: back to front, left to right, top to bottom, far to near, and so on.
   - Use spatial order expressions to show the order. Examples of spatial order expressions are *on the dashboard of my car*, *in front of the sofa*, and *in the distance*.

2. Unity is an important element of a good paragraph. Unity means that a paragraph discusses one, and only one, main idea.

3. Supporting details are the "meat" of a paragraph. They prove the truth of your topic sentence, and they make your writing rich and interesting.

4. *For*, *yet*, and *nor* are three additional coordinating conjunctions that you can use to make compound sentences.

5. One way to make your writing more interesting is to vary your sentence openings. Occasionally move a prepositional phrase to the beginning of a sentence. (You cannot move every prepositional phrase, however.)

6. Clustering is another prewriting technique you can use to get ideas.

Skill Sharpeners

The following exercises will help you review important skills you learned in prior chapters.

EXERCISE 1

Commas

Add commas where they are required in the following paragraph.

A Beach Treasure

¹Last Sunday my friend and I were walking along the beach and spotted an interesting shell on top of the sand. ²We stopped knelt down picked it up and brushed the sand from its surface. ³It was a disk about 3 inches in diameter with five V-shaped notches around its outer edge. ⁴It was round flat and gray-white in color. ⁵It was large for a sea shell yet it weighed almost nothing. ⁶I held it up to my nose and sniffed the salty smell of the ocean. ⁷On the top side of the disk Mother Nature had punched tiny holes in the shape of a flower with five petals. ⁸The other side of the disk was very plain for it had only one small hole in the center. ⁹At first we thought the shell was empty but we were wrong. ¹⁰We shook it and a stream of sand fell out. ¹¹Later we did a little research and learned that it wasn't a shell at all. ¹²It was the skeleton of an ocean animal. Do you know what this animal is?[1] (See the bottom of the page for the answer.)

EXERCISE 2

Summary Writing

Write a summary of "The Stairway" (page 61). Imagine that you are telling a friend the story. Include the important information, but write as few sentences as possible. Write no more than five sentences. Use these questions to pick out the important points.

1. What is the topic of this descriptive paragraph?
2. Where is the child when he describes the topic?
3. What part of the house does he describe? How does it appear to him?
4. What is at the top of the stairway?
5. How does he describe her?
6. What did he imagine then? What does he know now?

---

[1]The animal is a sand dollar.

Writing Assignment

Write a descriptive paragraph. Follow the steps in the writing process.

Step 1 Prewrite to get ideas. Use the clustering exercise that you completed in the Try It Out! exercise on page 73.

Step 2 Organize the ideas. Decide what kind of spatial order you will use. Make an outline. Include as many descriptive details as you can think of.

Step 3 Write the rough draft. Write ROUGH DRAFT at the top of your paper.

- Begin with a topic sentence that names the place and gives a general impression.
- Use spatial order.
- Include descriptive details to make your description lively and interesting.
- Write a concluding sentence.
- Pay attention to your sentence structure. Write both simple and compound sentences, and punctuate them correctly.

Step 4 Polish the rough draft.

- Exchange papers with a classmate and ask him or her to check your rough draft using Peer-Editing Worksheet 4 on page 204. Then discuss the completed worksheet and decide what changes you should make. Write a second draft.
- Use Self-Editing Worksheet 4 on page 205 to check your second draft for grammar, punctuation, and sentence structure.

Step 5 Write a final copy. Hand in your rough draft, your second draft, your final copy, and the page containing the two editing worksheets. Your teacher may also ask you to hand in your prewriting paper.

CHAPTER 5 · Logical Division of Ideas

Organization

Logical Division of Ideas

Coherence

Using Nouns and Pronouns Consistently

Transition Signals

Sentence Structure

Run-Ons and Comma Splices

Review

Writing Assignment

Organization

In this chapter, you will learn how to organize a paragraph using the **logical division of ideas** pattern. In the model paragraph, the writer discusses three reasons she does not own a credit card. As you read the paragraph, notice the word or phrase that signals each reason.

MODEL

Logical Division of Ideas Paragraph

Why I Don't Have a Credit Card

[1]There are three reasons I don't have a credit card. [2]The first reason is that using a piece of plastic instead of cash makes it too easy for me to buy things I can't afford. [3]For instance, last week I saw a $75.00 pair of pink sandals in my favorite shoe store. [4]Of course, I don't need pink sandals, nor can I afford them. [5]With a credit card, however, I would now own those sandals and be worrying about how to pay for them. [6]The second reason I don't have a credit card is that I would end up in debt[1] like my friend Sara the Shopaholic.[2] [7]Sara got a credit card last year, and she already owes $4,000. [8]She buys things that she doesn't really need, such as jewelry and designer sunglasses. [9]Sara makes only minimum payments each month. [10]Her monthly interest charges are more than her payments, so her balance[3] never decreases. [11]She will be in debt for years. [12]The third reason I don't have a credit card is the difficulty in understanding the fine print[4] in the credit card contract. [13]If I don't read the fine print, I can be surprised. [14]For example, some credit card companies will raise my interest rate if I make a payment even one day late. [15]To sum up, credit cards may be a convenience for some people, but for me, they are a plastic ticket to financial disaster.

Questions on the Model
1. How many reasons does the writer give for not having a credit card? Which sentence tells you the number?
2. Circle the words and phrases that signal each new reason.
3. How does the writer support each reason?

---

[1]**end up in debt:** find myself in the situation of owing a lot of money
[2]**shopaholic:** person who shops too often and buys too much
[3]**balance:** total amount owed
[4]**the fine print:** important details in a legal document that are often printed in smaller letters than the rest of the document and are therefore more difficult to read

Logical Division of Ideas

Logical division of ideas is a pattern of organization in which you divide a topic into points and discuss each point separately. The model paragraph uses this pattern. You can use logical division to organize many kinds of topics, not just reasons.

Sample Topics

- **reasons** for owning an iPod/cell phone/PDA/small automobile, for exercising/not exercising, for learning English, for IMing instead of making a phone call, for being a vegetarian . . .
- **kinds** of teachers/shoppers/drivers/friends/students/teachers/bosses/foods . . .
- **types** of books/movies/music/TV programs I like/don't like . . .
- **advantages** of living in a small town/big city/college dormitory, of being an only/the youngest/the oldest child/a twin . . .
- **disadvantages** of living in a small town/big city/college dormitory, of being an only/the youngest/the oldest child/a twin . . .
- **qualities** of a good boss/good employee/good friend/teacher/parent/nurse/ paramedic/salesperson . . .

Begin a logical division paragraph with a topic sentence similar to the following.

A good boss has three qualities.

Living in a college dormitory has several advantages.

There are four main styles of Chinese food.

In the supporting sentences, discuss each point one after the other. Introduce each new point with a signal word or phrase such as *The first reason . . .* , *The second type . . .* , *The final advantage . . .* , *In addition*, *Furthermore*, *Also*, and *Moreover*.

The first reason I am a vegetarian is that vegetarians are healthier than meat-eaters.

Another quality of a good boss is fairness.

In addition, sharing clothing with a twin saves money.

Support each point with a convincing detail such as an example or a statistic (numbers—costs, amounts, percentages, and so on).

For example, they want to touch and feel fabrics and visualize themselves in clothes.

She buys things that she doesn't really need, such as jewelry and designer sunglasses.

In 2005, there were thirteen major hurricanes in the North Atlantic.

A Big Mac contains 560 calories and 30 grams of fat.

End a logical division paragraph with a concluding sentence similar to one of these.

For all these reasons, living at home is the best choice for me at this time in my life.

To sum up, a champion has to be motivated, disciplined, and talented.

In brief, an effective ad grabs your attention and appeals to your emotions.

PRACTICE 1
*Recognizing
Logical Division*

Look through the paragraphs that are used as examples and practices in this chapter. Find at least three paragraphs that use logical division of ideas as a pattern of organization. *Hint*: Look for signal words and phrases that show divisions of a topic, such as *The first . . .* , *Another . . .* , and *In addition*.

Try It Out!

Choose one of the sample topics listed on page 78. Use listing, clustering, or freewriting to get ideas about the topic. Find at least three points and one example for each point. Then make an outline.

Coherence

In addition to unity, which you learned about in Chapter 4, every good paragraph must have **coherence**. A coherent paragraph flows smoothly from beginning to end. A reader can follow your ideas easily because one sentence leads naturally to the next one; there are no sudden jumps.

There are three main ways to make your paragraph coherent:

1. Use nouns and pronouns consistently throughout a paragraph.
2. Use transition signals to show relationships among ideas.
3. Put your ideas into some kind of logical order, such as logical division of ideas.

**Using Nouns
and Pronouns
Consistently**

One way to achieve coherence is to use nouns and pronouns **consistently** throughout a paragraph, that is, continue to use the same nouns and pronouns you start with. For example, if you begin with a plural noun such as *students*, don't change to singular. Also, don't change pronouns; don't switch from *you* to *they* or *he* for no reason. Be consistent! If you use the pronoun *you* at the beginning of your paragraph, keep it throughout.

Notice how nouns and pronouns in the following paragraph have been changed to make them consistent.

Word Roots

Students   Know   have
A student who knows a few Latin and Greek word roots has an advantage
     students   don't
over a student who doesn't know them. They can often guess the meaning
                       they
of unfamiliar words. If, for example, you know that the Latin word root *circum-*
          they
means "around," you can guess the meaning of words such as *circumference*,
                    they
circumvent, *circumstance*, and *circumnavigate* when you read them in a
sentence. Similarly, the Greek word root *mon-* or *mono-*, which means "one,
                     Students
single, alone," appears in dozens of English words. A student armed with this
knowledge can often discover the meanings of new words such as *monocle*,
monarchy, *monotone*, *monologue*, and *monolingual* without getting help from
       They
a dictionary. You also might be able to figure out that a monorail is a train that
uses one rail.

Here's a tip to help you use pronouns consistently.

Use a plural noun (*employees*) rather than a singular noun (*an employee*) when writing about a group of people of both sexes. When you need to use pronouns, the plural pronouns *they*, *them*, and *their* are less awkward than the singular phrases *he or she*, *him or her*, and *his or hers*.

AWKWARD   An employee must wear his or her ID badge at all times.

BETTER   Employees must wear their ID badges at all times.

PRACTICE 2

Consistent Pronouns

A. Circle the noun that is the topic of the paragraph and all pronouns that refer to it.

Some researchers believe that social animals such as dogs may have a sense of morality. That is, dogs know right from wrong. For example, dogs follow certain rules when they play together, and they exclude dogs that don't follow the rules. Dogs' sense of right and wrong also includes knowing how to behave correctly around humans. For example, they know who the pack leader (that is, the boss) in any family is. They also know that they are not allowed to eat the pack leader's food. If they steal a bite of food from Dad's dinner plate, they slink[1] around the kitchen looking guilty because they know they have broken a rule. Other researchers say that fear of punishment, not guilt, is the reason for dogs' slinking behavior.

B. Edit the following paragraphs for consistent nouns and pronouns.

Paragraph 1

A marathon runner must be strong not only in body but also in mind. She or he has to train for years to achieve the necessary endurance to compete in his or her sport. This requires great discipline and self-sacrifice. In addition, marathon runners have to train their minds in order to endure the long hours of solitary running. This, too, requires great discipline. In other words, you must be in top condition, both mentally and physically, if you want to run in marathons.

Paragraph 2

Physicists are scientists who study the basic laws of nature and apply these laws to improve the world. They are concerned with scientific wonders as large as the universe and as small as an electron. He or she is a problem solver who is curious about the universe and who is interested in what gives it order and meaning.

_____

[1]**slink:** walk quietly, head down, trying not to be noticed

Paragraph 3

Many students feel that learning to write well is a useless, time-consuming task that has little to do with "real life"— that is, with their future occupations. Although this may be true if he or she plans to become an auto mechanic or a waitress, it is certainly not true if you plan to have a white-collar job.[2] No matter what profession you enter — business, engineering, government, education — you will have to write.

Transition Signals

Another way to give a paragraph coherence is to use transition signals. **Transition signals** are words and phrases that connect the idea in one sentence with the idea in another sentence. They are expressions such as *first/second*, *furthermore*, *on the other hand*, *for example*, and *in conclusion*. Transition signals are like traffic signals; they tell your reader when to slow down, turn around, and stop. Using transition signals makes your paragraph smoother and helps your reader understand it more easily.

You have already used several transition signals. You practiced using time order signals in Chapter 2 and spatial order signals in Chapter 4. In Chapter 3, you learned the three signals for examples. In this chapter, you will practice using others.

Read and compare the following two paragraphs. Is 1 or 2 easier to understand? Why?

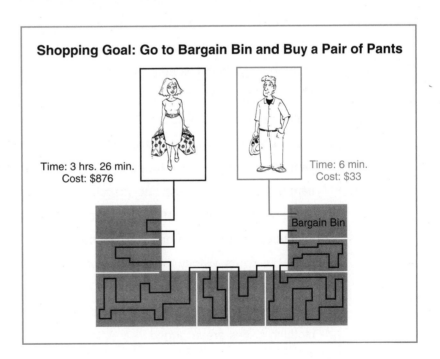

_____

[2]**white-collar job:** job in a bank, office, store, and so on, as opposed to a job as a factory worker, carpenter, plumber, auto mechanic, and so on.

Paragraph 1

Men and Women Shoppers

Store owners who understand the differences between men and women shoppers can use this knowledge to design their stores. Women shoppers use their five senses when they shop. They want to touch and feel fabrics and visualize[1] themselves in clothes. Owners of women's clothing shops place clothes with lots of frills[2] and luxury fabrics at the front of the shop. They place items near one another to allow a woman to visualize them together as an outfit. They group clothes not by item but by style — classic or casual, for instance. Men shoppers shop quite differently. Men shop for clothes only when they have to. A man buys a pair of jeans because his old ones have worn out. He probably wants exactly the same jeans. Men want everything in its place so that they can buy what they want and leave. They want all shirts together over here and all pants together over there. Men's clothing stores are arranged very differently from women's.

Paragraph 2

Men and Women Shoppers

Store owners who understand the differences between men and women shoppers can use this knowledge to design their stores. First of all, women shoppers use their five senses when they shop. For example, they want to touch and feel fabrics and visualize themselves in clothes. Therefore, owners of women's clothing shops place clothes with lots of frills and luxury fabrics at the front of the shop. Furthermore, they place items near one another to allow a woman to visualize them together as an outfit. They also group clothes not by item but by style — classic or casual, for instance. Men shoppers, on the other hand, shop quite differently. Men shop for clothes only when they have to. For instance, a man buys a pair of jeans because his old ones have worn out. He probably wants exactly the same jeans. Moreover, men want everything in its place so that they can buy what they want quickly and leave. They want all shirts together over here and all pants together over there. As a result, men's clothing stores are arranged very differently from women's.

Paragraph 2 is easier to read and understand because the writer has used transition signals. Each transition signal shows the relationship of one idea to the next.

---

[1]**visualize:** see in one's mind; imagine
[2]**frills:** decorations

- *First of all* tells you to look for the first main point.
- *For example* tells you to look for an example of the previous point.
- *Therefore* tells you that this is a result.
- *Furthermore* and *moreover* tell you to look for another similar idea.
- *On the other hand* tells you to look for a contrasting or opposite idea.
- *For instance* also tells you to look for an example.
- *As a result* tells you to look for a consequence of the previous point.

Let's review those you know and learn a few new ones. You will also learn new ways to use them.

Transition Signals

Sentence Connectors	Coordinating Conjunctions	Others
To list ideas in time order		
First, Second, First of all, Next, Meanwhile, After that, Finally, Now Soon Then		
To list ideas in logical division of ideas order		
First, Second, etc. First of all, Furthermore, Also, In addition, Moreover,	and	A second (reason, kind, advantage, etc.) . . . An additional (reason, kind, advantage, etc.) . . . The final (reason, kind, advantage, etc.) . . .
To add a similar idea		
Similarly, Likewise, Also, Furthermore, In addition, Moreover,	and	
To add an opposite idea		
On the other hand, However,	but	

(continued on next page)

Transition Signals   *(continued)*

Sentence Connectors	Coordinating Conjunctions	Others
To give an example		
For example, For instance,		such as (+ noun)
To give a reason		
	for	because of (+ noun)
To give a result		
Therefore, Thus, Consequently, As a result,	so	
To add a conclusion		
All in all, For these reasons, In brief, In conclusion, To summarize, To sum up,		It is clear that . . . You can see that . . . You can see from these examples that . . . These examples show that . . .

Following are some general rules for placing and punctuating these transition signals:

1. The words and phrases in the "Sentence Connectors" column often come at the beginning of a sentence. They are usually followed by a comma. (Exceptions: *Now*, *soon*, and *then* do not need a comma.)

BEGINNING OF SENTENCE   **First of all,** zoos protect animals from their natural enemies.

In short, advertising helps both buyers and sellers.

Then press the tab key on your keyboard.

Sentence connectors can also come in the middle and at the end of a sentence. We usually (but not always) separate them from the rest of the sentence with a comma or commas.

MIDDLE OF SENTENCE   Some people, **on the other hand,** object to keeping wild animals in cages.

You can **also** use keyboard shortcuts to type foreign letters and symbols. *(No comma between two parts of a verb phrase)*

END OF SENTENCE   They are protected and can live without risk of being attacked, **therefore.**

Anti-zoo groups say that wild animals do not reproduce well in captivity, **for example.**

2. Use the words in the "Coordinating Conjunctions" column to connect two simple sentences to make a compound sentence. Put a comma after the first simple sentence.

> All their needs are taken care of, **so** most zoo animals are healthy and contented.

3. The words in the "Others" column are adjectives and prepositions. They have no special punctuation.

> The **first** characteristic of a good politician is skill at public speaking.

> **Another** type of advertisement is aimed at children.

> Some people enjoy dangerous sports **such as** bungee-jumping and skydiving.

PRACTICE 3

Transition Signals

A. Add the appropriate transition signals from each list to the following paragraphs, and capitalize and punctuate them correctly. Do not use the same transition signal more than once (except in paragraph 3).

1. To list ideas in time order:

first (of all)	then
after that	next
second, third, etc.	finally

To apply for a scholarship, follow these steps. (a) _____ get an application form from your college's scholarship office. (b) _____ fill it out completely and accurately. (c) _____ ask two of your instructors to write letters of recommendation for you. (d) _____ turn in the application form and letters to the scholarship office before the deadline.

2. To add a similar idea:

and	moreover
also	in addition

Today it is possible to get many services without making human contact. For instance, you can buy music, rent movies, and order groceries online without speaking to a salesperson. (a) _____ you can buy almost anything from potato chips to underwear from vending machines that will accept your money and return change automatically. (b) _____ by using your cell phone, you can make national and international calls (c) _____ send text messages without operator assistance. You can (d) _____ earn college credits by taking online courses instead of going to class.

3. To give an example (*Note:* Use one signal twice.):

    for example   such as

        Children are motivated to learn if they are allowed to be successful.
No matter how small their progress is, each step helps to develop their
self-confidence (a) _____ when children master math concepts
(b) _____ addition and subtraction, they are more willing to attempt
more difficult concepts (c) _____ long division.

B. In the following paragraph, choose an appropriate transition signal from those
listed under each blank and write it in the blank. Capitalize and punctuate
correctly. In some cases, there may be more than one appropriate answer.

How Storms Are Named

    Have you ever
wondered how those big
ocean storms called
hurricanes or typhoons get
their names? Who decides
to name a hurricane *Ann*
or *Barbara* or *Bill*? The way
hurricanes and typhoons are named has changed over the years, and it is an
interesting story. Originally, weather forecasters described them by their position in
degrees of latitude and longitude (1) _____ a typhoon
                                      in addition / for example / but

might have been called *21.20 north, 157.52 west* (2) _____ this
                                      then / however / moreover

method was confusing because storms don't stay in the same place

(3) _____ people developed other ways to identify them. In
    thus / therefore / in brief

the Caribbean Sea, hurricanes were named for the Catholic saints' days

(4) _____ a hurricane that struck an island in the
    thus / for instance / moreover

Caribbean on Saint Ann's Day was named *Santa Ana*. During World War I,

hurricanes and typhoons were named according to the military alphabet: *Able,*

Baker, Charlie, and so on. During World War II, women's names began to be

used (5) _____ for the next thirty-five years, weather forecasters
        so / therefore / and

talked about *Typhoon Alice* or *Hurricane Betsy* (6) _____ in the
        however / then / also

1970s, the women's liberation movement came along and forced weather

forecasters to use men's names, too. (7) _____ after about
        thus / as a result / finally

1975, a storm could be named *Gertrude* or *George*. Currently, men's and

women's names alternate: *Alice, Bret, Carla, David, Ellen, Frederick*, and so on.

(8) _____, the way hurricanes and typhoons are named has
        to sum up / so / as a result

changed over the years and will undoubtedly change again.

Caution!
Do not overuse transition signals. Using too many is just as confusing as using too few. Don't use a transition signal in every sentence. Use one only when it helps your reader understand how one sentence relates to another sentence.

Sentence Structure

Run-Ons and Comma Splices

In Chapter 1, you learned about a sentence error called a *fragment*, or *incomplete sentence*. In this chapter, you will learn about two sentence errors, **run-ons** and **comma splices**.

Run-ons and comma splices are similar errors. Both happen when you join sentences incorrectly.

A run-on happens when you join two simple sentences without a comma and without a connecting word.

RUN-ON
Men like to shop quickly women like to browse.[1]

A comma splice error happens when you join two simple sentences with a comma alone.

COMMA SPLICE
Men like to shop quickly, women like to browse.

There are three easy ways to correct run-on and comma splice errors.[2]

1. Join the two sentences with a comma and a coordinating conjunction such as *and*, *but*, or *so*.

Men like to shop quickly, but women like to browse.

---

[1]**browse:** look at many items in a store without buying anything
[2]Other ways to correct run-ons and comma splices use semicolons. Semicolons are not taught in this book.

2. Make two sentences. Separate the two sentences with a period.

> Men like to shop quickly. Women like to browse.

3. If you wish to show the relationship between the two sentences, add a sentence connector (and a comma) to the second sentence.

> Men like to shop quickly. However, women like to browse.

Correcting run-ons and comma splices is relatively easy. Finding them is often the real challenge. Here are three tips to help you recognize run-ons and comma splices.

1. Check all sentences that have a comma in the middle.

COMMA SPLICE
> My best subject is computer science, my worst subject is English.

What is the first subject in this sentence? What verb goes with it? Read further. Is there another subject with its own verb? If the answer is yes, look for a coordinating conjunction. If there is none, then this is a run-on sentence.

CORRECTION
> My best subject is computer science. My worst subject is English.
>> OR
> My best subject is computer science, and my worst subject is English.

2. Read a long sentence aloud. Sometimes reading aloud helps you to recognize where a new sentence should begin.

RUN-ON
> Advertising is a multibillion-dollar industry in the United States more than $200 billion is spent on advertising and advertising-related activities each year.

When you read the sentence aloud, do you pause between *United States* and *more*? *More* is the first word of a new sentence.

CORRECTION
> Advertising is a multibillion-dollar industry in the United States. More than $200 billion is spent on advertising and advertising-related activities each year.

3. Look for words like *then*, *also*, and *therefore* in the middle of a sentence. These words are "danger words" because they frequently occur in run-on sentences.

COMMA SPLICE
> We drove into the city, then we spent thirty minutes looking for a place to park.

CORRECTION
> We drove into the city, and then we spent thirty minutes looking for a place to park.
>> OR
> We drove into the city and spent thirty minutes looking for a place to park.
>> OR
> We drove into the city. Then we spent thirty minutes looking for a place to park.

PRACTICE 4

*Editing for
Sentence Errors*

A. Read each sentence and decide if it is a run-on or comma splice or if it is correct. Write *X* on the line next to the errors. Then correct each sentence that you marked.

___X___ 1. Alicia and Marta are a lot alike, they both have dark hair and eyes.

Alicia and Marta are a lot alike. They both have dark hair and eyes.

_____ 2. Both women are single, but Marta has a boyfriend.

_____ 3. Writing a paragraph is easy it takes practice.

_____ 4. First, you write a topic sentence, then you make an outline of the supporting sentences.

_____ 5. In high school, I never studied, but now I work hard.

_____ 6. College is not like high school it is a lot harder.

_____ 7. I want to transfer to a four-year college, so I try to get good grades.

_____ 8. My parents did not finish high school, I was the first member of my family to graduate.

_____ 9. In the old days, people did not have the opportunity to attend school, they had to work to help support the family.

_____ 10. Now parents want a better future for their children, they encourage them to go to college and even help them achieve that goal.

(continued on next page)

B. Find and circle errors in sentence structure and punctuation in the following paragraph. Look for run-on and comma splice errors. Then correct the errors. (*Note*: There may be more than one way to correct some of the errors.)

Ways of Cooking Rice

[1]There are hundreds of different kinds of rice and hundreds of different ways to cook it. [2]The kind of rice eaten daily in most Asian countries is sticky rice. [3]Asian sticky rice is rinsed, soaked, cooked, and then steamed, the lid remains on the cooking pot during the entire cooking and steaming process. [4]When the rice is ready to eat, the grains are soft and fluffy, and they stick together. [5]Asian cooks never stir rice while it is cooking. [6]Italian cooks, on the other hand, stir the pot constantly when they make *risotto*.[1] [7]*Risotto* has a creamy texture, the individual grains have a chewy center. [8]Persian rice is quite different it has a golden, crunchy crust. [9]Thai people serve jasmine rice, and people in India enjoy basmati rice, both kinds have a special perfume-like aroma. [10]Indeed, rice is one of the most versatile[2] foods in the world.

Review

These are the important points covered in this chapter:

1. Logical division of ideas is a pattern of organizing ideas in which you divide a topic into parts and discuss each part separately.

2. A paragraph needs coherence. A coherent paragraph is easy to read because it flows smoothly from beginning to end. Use these three techniques to achieve coherence.

   • Use nouns and pronouns consistently.
   • Use transition signals to show how one idea is related to the next.
   • Put your ideas into some kind of logical order.

3. Run-ons and comma splices are sentence errors in which you join two sentences incorrectly.

---

[1]**risotto:** Italian dish made with rice, broth, and cheese
[2]**versatile:** having many different uses

Skill Sharpeners

The following exercises will help you review important skills you learned in prior chapters.

EXERCISE 1
Unity

Read the following paragraph. Find and cross out one sentence that breaks the unity of the paragraph.

Secrets of Good Ads

¹A good ad has three characteristics. ²First of all, a good ad is simple. ³It lets pictures, not words, tell the story. ⁴Of course, all ads need some words, but a good ad has a powerful headline and only a small amount of text. ⁵Second, a good ad is directed to a particular group of consumers. ⁶For example, ads for face creams are for older women, and ads for motorcycles are for unmarried young men. ⁷Third, a good ad appeals to emotions. ⁸Women in the thirty-to-fifty age group, for instance, want to look and feel younger, so face cream ads tell them that women who use XYZ face cream will look like the twenty-year-old models pictured in the ad. ⁹Teenagers want to feel popular, so ads directed at teens often show a happy, confident-looking group of young people using the product in the ad. ¹⁰Teenagers have a surprising amount of money to spend, so advertisers research teenage fads and fashions. ¹¹In conclusion, good ads are simple, are directed at a specific group, and make an emotional connection.

EXERCISE 2
Outlining

Outline the paragraph "Secrets of Good Ads." Omit the sentence you crossed out in the preceding practice.

EXERCISE 3
Summary Writing

Write a summary of the model paragraph at the beginning of this chapter, "Why I Don't Have a Credit Card," on page 77.

Writing Assignment

Use the outline you prepared for the Try It Out! exercise on page 79 and write a paragraph. Use logical division of ideas as a pattern of organization.

You have already completed Steps 1 and 2 of the writing process.

Step 3 Write a rough draft. Write ROUGH DRAFT at the top of your paper.

- Begin your paragraph with a topic sentence for logical division of ideas similar to the examples on page 78.
- Use examples or other kinds of details to support your points.

- Use transition signals to show the divisions of your topic.
- Pay attention to sentence structure. Write both simple and compound sentences, and punctuate them correctly.

Step 4 Polish the rough draft.

- Exchange papers with a classmate and ask him or her to check your rough draft using Peer-Editing Worksheet 5 on page 206. Then discuss the completed worksheet and decide what changes you should make. Write a second draft.
- Use Self-Editing Worksheet 5 on page 207 to check your second draft for grammar, punctuation, and sentence structure.

Step 5 Write a final copy. Hand in your rough draft, your second draft, your final copy, and the page containing the two editing worksheets. Your teacher may also ask you to hand in your prewriting paper.

Alternative Writing Assignment

Become a restaurant reviewer. Write a one-paragraph review of a restaurant in your area.

You may want to work with another student or in a small group to develop ideas for your restaurant review. (Each student should write his or her own review, however, because you may want to write about different points.)

Use the Restaurant Reviewer's Notebook form on the next page to make notes and organize information. Your review is only one paragraph, so do not use all the points suggested on the form. Choose no more than three points, such as food, service, prices, or decor, to write about. Once you have decided on your points and examples, make an outline. Then complete steps 3, 4, and 5 in the preceding Writing Assignment.

Begin your review with a topic sentence that names the restaurant and makes a general statement about it.

> Papa Joe's has the best pizza in the city.

> For a delicious but inexpensive meal, try Alice's Restaurant.

In the supporting sentences, discuss each point separately. Use at least one specific example to support each point.

> Second, the prices are reasonable. For example, a large vegetarian pizza costs just $8.00.

End your review with a recommendation: Should people go to the restaurant, and why (or why not)? Summarize the points in your review.

> For great pizza, go to Papa Joe's, but expect slow service.

> To sum up, you get good food at cheap prices at Alice's Restaurant.

Restaurant Reviewer's Notebook		
Restaurant Name		
Restaurant Address		
		Number of Stars[1]
Location (easy to find? parking available?)		
Interior (clean? noisy? pleasant décor?)		
Food		
Service (efficient? friendly?)		
Prices		

[1]Give your restaurant 0–5 stars. Excellent *****   Very good ****   Average ***   Below Average ** Poor *   Don't eat here (☹)

6 Process Paragraphs

Organization
  Time Order
    Time Order Signals

Sentence Structure
  Clauses
  Complex Sentences

Review

Writing Assignment

Organization

In a **process paragraph**, you explain how to make or do something, so process paragraphs are also called *how-to paragraphs*. To explain how to do something clearly, break the process down into a series of steps and explain each step.

The model paragraph explains the process of building a campfire. As you read it, count the number of steps. Also, notice the words and phrases that introduce each step.

MODEL

Process Paragraph

How to Build a One-Match Campfire

¹Building a campfire that you can light with one match is simple if you follow these easy steps. ²The first step is to prepare a safe place for your campfire. ³Clear an area on the ground at least 3 feet wide, and put a circle of stones around it. ⁴Second, gather fuel. ⁵You will need several sizes of fuel: small twigs, medium sticks, and large sticks. ⁶The next step is to build a tepee.¹ ⁷Put a handful of twigs in a small pile, and use the small sticks to build a small tepee over the pile. ⁸Leave spaces large enough to drop a lighted match through. ⁹Next, build a cabin² around the tepee using the medium sticks. ¹⁰Fifth, place two large pieces of wood on either side of the cabin, and lay two or three long sticks on top to make a loose roof. ¹¹The last step is to light a match and drop it through a space in the tepee. ¹²Soon you will enjoy the warmth of a nice fire, and your friends will admire your skill at lighting a campfire with only one match!

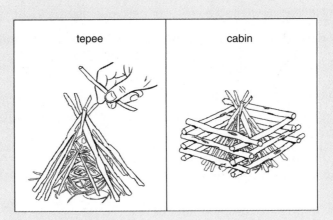

tepee   cabin

Questions on the Model
1. Underline the topic sentence. What words tell the reader that the paragraph will explain a process?
2. How many steps are there?
3. Does the concluding sentence summarize the steps, or does it restate the topic sentence in different words?

---

¹**tepee:** cone-shaped "house" used by some Native Americans
²**cabin:** small house made of wood

A process paragraph begins with a topic sentence that names the topic and tells the reader to look for a process or procedure. Use words such as *steps*, *procedure*, *directions*, *suggestions*, and *instructions*.

> You can teach your dog to fetch[1] in a very short time by following this procedure.
>
> Making a pizza is easy if you follow these instructions.
>
> Follow these steps to throw a Frisbee[2] accurately.

The supporting sentences are the steps and details about each step.

> When your dog brings back the stick, praise him extravagantly.
>
> The first step is to gather the ingredients you will need.
>
> First, grip the edge of the Frisbee with all your fingers wrapped underneath the edge and your thumb along the top.

The concluding sentence can be the last step, or it can give the results.

> At the end of the lesson, give your dog a nice treat for a job well done.
>
> Now sit down and enjoy your delicious pizza.
>
> Finally, make sure the Frisbee stays level while you throw.

PRACTICE 1

Topic Sentences for Process Paragraphs

Work with a partner or with a small group. Write a topic sentence for four of the following topics. You may want to use one of these topics for your paragraph at the end of this chapter.

how to register for classes at your school
how to meet people in a new place
how to get the job of your dreams
how to prepare for a job interview
how to live on a tight budget
how to make ceviche, sushi, satay, egg rolls, dulce de leche, or any dish popular in your culture
how to make a piñata, a confetti egg, a decorated egg, a May basket, a paper flower, or any craft item
how to change the oil in a car, change a flat tire, build a kite, catch a fish or a crab, or any other skill

---

[1]**fetch:** go after an object such as a stick or ball and bring it back
[2]**Frisbee:** piece of plastic shaped like a plate that you throw to someone else as a game

Time Order

In a process paragraph, you arrange the steps in order by time and use time order signals to guide your reader from step to step.

You are already familiar with time order signals from Chapter 2. Here are others:

Time Order Signals

Sentence Connectors	Others
1. First, (Second, etc.) Then (no comma) Now (no comma) Next, Finally, After that, Meanwhile,	2. The first step . . . (no comma) The next step . . . (no comma) The final step . . . (no comma) 3. After five minutes, 4. After you take the pizza out of the oven,

1. **First,** preheat the oven to 500 degrees Fahrenheit.
   Then prepare the pizza sauce.
2. **The next step** is to mix the pizza dough.
3. **After five minutes,** check the pizza.
4. **After you take the pizza out of the oven,** cut it into 8 pieces.

Notice that you can also use time clauses to show time order, as in example 4 above. Learn about time clauses in the Sentence Structure section on pages 99–104 of this chapter.

PRACTICE 2

Time Order Signals

A. Turn back to the model on page 95. Draw a circle around all the time order signals you find.

B. Complete the paragraph with the time order signals and add commas if necessary: Use each signal once. Use these time order signals: *Finally*, *The third step*, *To sum up*, *Second*, *The first step*.

Choosing Classes

Choosing the right classes each semester can be stressful, but you can reduce your stress by following these steps. (1) _The first step_ is to become familiar with the graduation requirements for your major. Do not depend on others to give you correct information. Instead, study the pages in the college bulletin[3] dealing with your major and memorize the requirements.

(2) _____ plan, plan, plan. Write out a program for each

(*continued on next page*)

---

[3]**college bulletin:** publication that contains important information for students

semester to make sure you have all the courses you need for graduation. Be aware that some classes have prerequisites — classes you must pass before you can register for them. (3) _____ is to talk with as many older students as you can. Ask them which courses are good and which ones are not. Don't waste your time and money on bad classes. (4) _____ register each semester as soon as you can. Waiting even an hour may mean that the classes you want or need are filled. (5) _____ plan ahead to avoid missing any required classes, to avoid bad classes, and to graduate on time.

C. The following sets of sentences are not in correct time order. Number the sentences (1, 2, 3, and so on) in the correct order.

1.   **How to Make Ice Cream in a Bag**

_____ Seal the gallon bag securely.
_____ Open the bags, grab a spoon, and enjoy your ice cream!
_____ Gently rock the gallon bag from side to side for ten to fifteen minutes or until the contents of the quart bag have turned into ice cream.
__2__ Put ½ cup of heavy cream, ½ cup of milk, ¼ cup of sugar, and ¼ teaspoon of vanilla into a quart-size sealable plastic bag.
_____ Close the quart-size bag and seal it tightly.
_____ Put 2 cups of ice and ½ to ¾ cup of salt into a gallon-size sealable plastic bag.
_____ Surprise your friends on your next camping trip by making ice cream in a plastic bag.
_____ Place the sealed quart bag inside the gallon bag of ice and salt.

2.   **How to Find a Book in the Library**

_____ Find the computers that contain the library's catalogs.
_____ Locate the books on the library shelves by their call numbers.
_____ Be prepared to show your library card at the checkout desk.
_____ In the age of computers, finding a book in a library has become very easy.
_____ In the book catalog, type the topic you are seeking information about in the space labeled "Subject."
_____ There are two catalogs: one for books and one for periodicals (magazines, newspapers, and so on).
_____ Write down the title and call number of each book that you want.
_____ Scroll through the entries for the books that are displayed on the computer screen, and determine which ones seem the most relevant.
_____ Take the books to the checkout desk.

Try It Out!   Write each group of sentences from the preceding exercise as a paragraph. Make your paragraphs flow smoothly by adding time order signal words or phrases at the beginning of some of the sentences.

Sentence Structure

MODEL

Clauses and Complex Sentences

How to Give the Cat a Pill

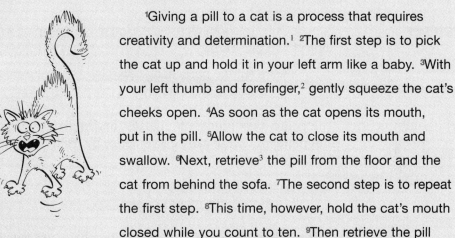

[1]Giving a pill to a cat is a process that requires creativity and determination.[1] [2]The first step is to pick the cat up and hold it in your left arm like a baby. [3]With your left thumb and forefinger,[2] gently squeeze the cat's cheeks open. [4]As soon as the cat opens its mouth, put in the pill. [5]Allow the cat to close its mouth and swallow. [6]Next, retrieve[3] the pill from the floor and the cat from behind the sofa. [7]The second step is to repeat the first step. [8]This time, however, hold the cat's mouth closed while you count to ten. [9]Then retrieve the pill from the goldfish bowl and the cat from behind the washing machine. [10]The third step is to call a neighbor for help. [11]When the neighbor arrives, ask him to hold the cat's body firmly between his knees and its head between his hands. [12]Then force open the cat's mouth with a wooden stick and push in the pill. [13]After that, retrieve the cat from the curtain rod, make a note to repair the curtains, and bandage your neighbor's hands. [14]Now get a new pill for a final attempt. [15]Tie the cat's four paws[4] together with strong rope, and tie the cat securely to the leg of the dining table. [16]After you put on heavy-duty gloves, hide the pill in a large piece of fish, push it into the cat's mouth, and pour in a quart of water to wash it all down. [17]On your way home from the emergency room (where the doctor sewed up your bleeding arm), order a new dining table and call the SPCA[5] to come get the cat.

---

[1]**determination:** trying to do something even though it is difficult
[2]**forefinger:** finger next to the thumb
[3]**retrieve:** find something and bring it back
[4]**paws:** feet of some animals, such as cats and dogs
[5]**SPCA:** Society for the Prevention of Cruelty to Animals, an organization that takes unwanted pets

Questions on the Model
1. Look at sentence 3. What is the verb? What kind of sentence is it—simple or compound? (*Note*: This sentence is a command. In commands, we understand that the subject is *you*, but *you* is not expressed.)
2. Find other simple sentences that are commands. How many can you find?
3. Look at sentence 8. How many SV combinations does it contain? What word connects them?

In previous chapters, you learned about simple sentences and compound sentences. In this chapter, you will study a third kind of sentence, called a *complex sentence*.

Clauses

First, let's learn about clauses. A **clause** is a group of words that contains at least one subject and one verb.

CLAUSES

Anna left the party early.
. . . because she was tired

There are two kinds of clauses in English: independent and dependent. An **independent clause** can be a sentence by itself. *Independent clause* is another name for simple sentence.

INDEPENDENT CLAUSES

Anna left the party early.
Hold the cat's mouth closed.

A **dependent clause**, in contrast, cannot be a sentence by itself because its meaning is not complete. A dependent clause "depends" on something else to complete its meaning.

DEPENDENT CLAUSES

. . . because she was tired
. . . while you count to ten

Complex Sentences

A **complex sentence** is a combination of one independent clause and one (or more) dependent clause(s).

┌──── INDEP. CLAUSE ────┐ ┌──── DEP. CLAUSE ────┐
Anna left the party early because she was tired.

┌──── INDEP. CLAUSE ────┐ ┌──── DEP. CLAUSE ────┐
Hold the cat's mouth closed while you count to ten.

Usually, the clauses can be in any order. However, the punctuation is different.

> **Comma Rule**
>
> In a complex sentence, when the dependent clause comes first, separate the clauses with a comma. When the independent clause comes first, do not separate them.
>
> Because she was tired, Anna left the party early.
>
> Anna left the party early because she was tired.

A dependent clause always begins with a subordinating word, or **subordinator**. There are different kinds of subordinators. Time subordinators begin a clause that tells *when* something happens. Reason subordinators begin a clause that tells *why* something happens. Place subordinators begin a clause that tells *where* something happens or where something is located.

Subordinators

Time Subordinators	
after	He goes to school **after** he finishes work.
as*	Several overcrowded buses passed **as** we were waiting.
as soon as	She felt better **as soon as** she took the medicine.
before	**Before** you apply to college, you have to take an entrance exam.
since	It has been a year **since** I left home.
until	We can't leave the room **until** everyone has finished the test.
when	**When** you start college, you sometimes have to take a placement test.
whenever	**Whenever** I don't sleep well, I feel sick the next day.
while	Several overcrowded buses passed **while** they were waiting.
Reason Subordinators	
because	Jack excels at sports **because** he trains hard.
since	**Since** she works out daily, Jill is in great condition.
as*	**As** they want to compete in a marathon, they run every day.
Place Subordinators	
where	I can never remember **where** I put my house keys.
wherever	A baby animal follows its mother **wherever** she goes.

*Notice that *as* can be either a time subordinator or a reason subordinator.

PRACTICE 3

Complex Sentences

A. Find and underline three complex sentences with time clauses in the model paragraph "How to Give the Cat a Pill," on page 99.

B. Identify the parts of the following complex sentence.

Step 1 Underline independent clauses with a solid line and dependent clauses with a broken line.

Step 2 Circle the subordinators.

Step 3 Add a comma if necessary.

Note: Two sentences have two dependent clauses.

1. (Whenever) astronauts leave Earth's atmosphere, they experience weightlessness.

2. Astronauts often feel seasick when they first experience weightlessness.

3. Astronauts must exercise on special machines while they are orbiting Earth in their spacecraft.

4. When the first Russian cosmonauts exited their spacecraft they had to be carried because they could not walk.

5. The students were silent as the teacher handed out the test.

6. The students worked on the test problems until the teacher told them to stop.

7. As soon as the teacher told them to stop writing they put down their pencils.

8. After the teacher collected the tests she dismissed the class.

9. Before she left she promised to post their scores[1] where students could view them.

10. Since noise can change the heart rate and increase blood pressure it is harmful to the body.

11. Loud noise is especially harmful as it damages the ear drums.

12. Rock musicians and construction workers can lose their hearing because they are exposed to loud noise over long periods of time.

C. Combine an independent clause from Column A with a dependent clause from Column B to make a complex sentence. Then write the sentences on a separate piece of paper in order as a paragraph. Punctuate each sentence correctly.

---

[1]**post their scores:** put a list of scores in a place where students can see them—on a bulletin board or on a web site, for example

In a book about animal morality, the author tells the following story.

A	B
1. during World War II, a British soldier got caught in a tree	a. while he hung helplessly in the trees
2. the monkey continued to bring him fruit	b. after he had parachuted into the jungles of Sumatra, Indonesia
3. the soldier finally succeeded in freeing himself	c. after twelve days had passed
4. however, he still had a problem	d. because it seemed to understand the problem and to want to help
5. a wild monkey brought him bananas and other fruit every day	e. as he had no way to contact his comrades

D. Write six complex sentences of your own. Use a different subordinator in each sentence. Write three sentences with the dependent clause first, and three sentences with the independent clause first.

Try It Out!

Work with a partner on this exercise.

Step 1 Combine the sentences in each group of sentences on the following page into one sentence. There is more than one way to combine some of them.

Step 2 Then write the sentences on a separate piece of paper as a connected paragraph, starting with the first sentence.

How Much Can Animals Think and Feel?

1. Scientists are discovering something.
   Animals can think.
   Animals can communicate their thoughts.
   (*Substitute the word* that *for* something.)
   <u>Scientists are discovering that animals can think and communicate their thoughts.</u>

2. Gorillas are close relatives of humans.
   Chimpanzees are close relatives of humans.
   Scientists have worked with them to study animal intelligence.

3. A young chimpanzee named Kanzi knows as much grammar as a two-and-a-half-year-old child.
   A gorilla named Koko uses sign language to communicate with her trainer.

4. Most people believe something.
   Parrots can only imitate.
   They don't understand what they are saying.
   (*Substitute the word* that *for* something.)

(continued on next page)

5. However, a parrot named Alex talks.
   He seems to understand what he is saying.

6. He can answer questions about the color of a toy.
   He can answer questions about the shape of a toy.
   He can answer questions about the size of a toy.
   He can tell what it is made of.

7. Furthermore, Alex can also feel.
   Alex can communicate his feelings.

8. Alex made several mistakes in answering a question.
   He apologized.
   He turned away.
   He did this one day. *(Put this idea first.)*
   <u>One day, when Alex . . .</u>

9. Alex became sick.
   His trainer had to leave him overnight in an animal hospital.
   This happened another time. *(Put this idea first.)*

10. The hospital was a strange place.
    Alex didn't want to stay there alone.

11. The trainer was going out the door.
    Alex cried out, "Come here. I love you. I'm sorry. Wanna go back."

12. Dolphins also show emotion.
    They do this during training.

13. They are correct.
    They cry excitedly.
    They race back to their trainer.

14. They are wrong.
    They look sad.
    They act depressed.

15. These few examples show something.
    Even animals with small brains are smart.
    Even animals with small brains have feelings.
    (Substitute the word that *for something.)*

Review

These are the important points covered in this chapter:

1. In a process paragraph, you explain how to do or make something.

   - Begin with a topic sentence that names the process and indicates a series of steps.
   - Organize the steps in order by time, and use time order signals and time clauses to guide your reader from step to step.

2. A clause is a group of words with a subject and a verb. There are two kinds of clauses: independent and dependent.

   - An independent clause can be a sentence by itself. An independent clause is another name for simple sentence.
   - A dependent clause begins with a subordinator and cannot be a sentence by itself.

3. There are subordinators that show time, reason, and place.

4. A complex sentence is one independent and at least one dependent clause.

5. The comma rule for complex sentences with time clauses is as follows:

   - When a dependent clause comes before an independent clause, separate the clauses with a comma.
   - When an independent clause comes before a dependent clause, do not separate them with a comma.

Skill Sharpeners

The following exercises will help you review important skills you learned in prior chapters.

EXERCISE 1

Comma

Add commas to the following paragraph wherever they are necessary.

How to Make Scrambled Eggs

[1]Scrambled eggs are a quick and easy light meal. [2]You need two fresh eggs milk butter salt and pepper. [3]You also need a mixing bowl a tablespoon a fork and a frying pan. [4]First break the eggs into the bowl. [5]Then add about three tablespoons of milk the salt and the pepper. [6]Beat the mixture with a fork until it is well mixed. [7]Next melt a small piece of butter in the frying pan over low heat. [8]Pour the egg mixture into the pan and let it heat through. [9]Then turn up the heat slightly. [10]As the eggs cook push them around gently with the fork. [11]When the scrambled eggs are done to perfection they should be light and fluffy. [12]In just a few minutes you can sit down and enjoy your delicious meal.

Find and correct five errors in sentence structure in the following paragraph. Look for fragments, comma splices, and run-ons.

A Traditional Hindu Wedding

¹A traditional Hindu wedding lasts all day and well into the night. ²On the day of the ceremony, one of the groom's brothers goes to the bride's home with gifts, these gifts seal the union of the two families. ³Then the groom arrives at the bride's home with his family and his friends. ⁴Dressed in rich¹ clothing and wearing a special headdress. ⁵He usually arrives in a white car or on a white horse, but he sometimes rides a white elephant. ⁶Then the wedding ceremony takes place. ⁷During the ceremony, the couple sits around a sacred fire under a special canopy.² ⁸A Hindu priest performs the ceremony by chanting special wedding prayers. ⁹After that, the bride's dress is tied to the groom's scarf, and they walk around the fire seven times. ¹⁰The groom makes seven promises. ¹¹To make his wife happy, to share his feelings with her, to share his possessions with her, to be faithful, to respect her family, and to make her a part of his life. ¹²The seventh promise is to keep the other six promises! ¹³The party begins after the ceremony. ¹⁴Musicians provide entertainment then a feast of traditional Indian food is served. ¹⁵During the party, the bride, the groom, and their guests play some traditional games. ¹⁶The party may go on until midnight, everyone is pretty tired at the end.

Cross out two sentences that break the unity of the paragraph.

How to Eat an Artichoke

¹Artichokes are vegetables that look like green pinecones but taste delicious. ²If you have never eaten one, you may not know how or where to start. ³Lobster is another food that is difficult to eat. ⁴Here's how to cook and eat an artichoke. ⁵First, cut off the stem with a knife. ⁶Then cut off the end of each leaf with scissors. ⁷Steam the whole artichoke in a pot of water until it is soft. ⁸To eat it, pull off one leaf at a time, hold the cut end, and dip the leaf into melted butter or mayonnaise. ⁹Then put the dipped end into your mouth. ¹⁰Pull the leaf through your teeth and scrape off the soft part. ¹¹Throw away the tough part. ¹²Continue doing this until all of the leaves are gone. ¹³Next, take a spoon, scrape out the

¹**rich:** beautiful, expensive
²**canopy:** tent without walls

fuzzy part in the center, and throw it away. ¹⁴A lobster also has parts that you don't eat.¹⁵The remaining part of the artichoke — the bottom — is the heart, which is the best part. ¹⁶Cut the heart into pieces, dip each piece into the sauce, and enjoy the delicious taste.

Writing Assignment

Choose one of the topics from Practice 1 on page 96 and write a paragraph. Follow the steps in the writing process.

Step 1 Prewrite to get ideas.

Step 2 Organize the ideas. Put the steps into time order by making a list of the steps or by making an outline of the steps.

Step 3 Write a rough draft. Write ROUGH DRAFT at the top of your paper.

- Use time order to organize your paragraph. Use time order word and clause signals and time clauses, and punctuate them correctly.
- Pay attention to your sentence structure. Write simple, compound, and complex sentences.

Step 4 Polish the rough draft.

- Exchange papers with a classmate and ask him or her to check your rough draft using Peer-Editing Worksheet 6 on page 208. Then discuss the completed worksheet and decide what changes you should make. Write a second draft.
- Use Self-Editing Worksheet 6 on page 209 to check your second draft for grammar, punctuation, and sentence structure.

Step 5 Write a final copy. Hand in your rough draft, your second draft, your final copy, and the page containing the two editing worksheets. Your teacher may also ask you to hand in your prewriting paper.

Alternative Writing Topics

Try using humor to write about some of these topics!

how to find/choose a marriage partner
how to propose (marriage)
how to lose 10 pounds in two days
how to grow a houseplant
how to kill a houseplant

how to drive a teacher crazy
describe a wedding or other
  important ceremony
explain the steps in the educational
  system where you live

Comparison/Contrast Paragraphs

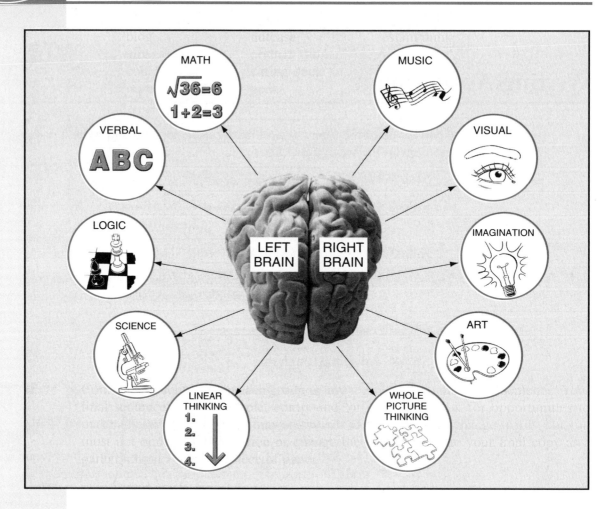

Organization
Block Organization
Point-by-Point Organization

Sentence Structure
Comparison Signals
Contrast Signals

Review

Writing Assignment

Organization

Comparison and contrast is a technique that we use every day. For example, we compare and contrast courses and teachers when we decide which classes to take. We compare and contrast products and prices when we shop. An employer compares and contrasts applicants for jobs, and a job applicant compares and contrasts job offers. In college classes, you will often have to compare and contrast. For example, in a history class, you might be asked to compare and contrast two historical figures or two events. In a literature class, you might have to compare two poems or two characters in a play. Knowing how to write comparison/contrast paragraphs is a very useful skill.

When we compare two (or more) things, we tell what is similar about them. When we contrast things, we tell what is different about them. Usually, the emphasis is on the differences, but sometimes a paragraph describes both similarities and differences. As you read the model paragraphs, decide which one emphasizes differences and which one describes both similarities and differences.

MODELS

Comparison/ Contrast Paragraphs

Paragraph 1

Right Brain / Left Brain

¹The left and right sides of your brain process information in different ways. ²The left side is logical, rational, linear, and verbal. ³The right side, on the other hand, processes information intuitively,¹ emotionally, creatively, and visually. ⁴Left brains think in words, whereas right brains think in pictures. ⁵People who depend more on the left side of their brain are list makers and analysts. ⁶They are detailed, careful, and organized. ⁷In contrast, right-brained people are visual, intuitive, and sensual. ⁸When a left-brained person has to make an important decision, he or she makes a mental list of all the factors involved and arrives at a decision only after careful analysis. ⁹When a right-brained person has to make the same decision, on the other hand, he or she is more likely to base it on intuition and feelings. ¹⁰For example, a left-brained automobile shopper will consider a car's cost, fuel efficiency, and resale value, whereas a right-brained shopper bases a decision on how shiny the chrome is, how soft the seats are, and how smoothly the car drives. ¹¹Of course, no one is 100 percent left-brained or 100 percent right-brained. ¹²Athough one side may be stronger, both sides normally work together.

---

¹**intuitively:** instinctively, without thinking

Read the following chart that the personnel manager for a medical laboratory prepared. In the chart, she summarized the qualifications of two applicants for a summer job as a receptionist in a medical laboratory. Then read the memo she wrote to her boss.

Two Job Applicants

	Applicant JZ	Applicant SW
education	high school graduate; 2 years college; 3.4 GPA[1]	high school graduate; 2 years college; 3.5 GPA
work history	summer job as a file clerk in doctor's office (some patient contact); volunteer in retirement home	summer jobs—car wash, pizza delivery, hospital volunteer (library, gift shop, no patient contact)
interview	excellent—friendly, open; likes to be part of a team.	excellent—friendly, open; likes to work independently
references check	excellent recommendation from one past employer	excellent recommendations from all past employers
availability	June 1	June 1

Paragraph 2

Miller Medical Labs
Memorandum

To: Director of Human Resources

From: Barbara Johnson, Interviewer

[1]From the fourteen applications received for the job of receptionist, two applicants stand out. [2]Following is a summary of their qualifications. [3]Educationally, the two applicants are quite similar. [4]JZ has completed two years of college, just as SW has, and their grade point averages are approximately equal. [5]JZ's one past employer was very positive. [6]Similarly, SW's past employers gave very high recommendations. [7]Finally, both applicants can start work on the same date (June 1). [8]There are two differences between the job applicants that may influence the hiring decision. [9]The first difference is that JZ's job in a medical office included some contact with patients, whereas SW's volunteer work in the library and gift shop of a local hospital included no patient contact. [10]Second, JZ likes to be part

---

[1]**GPA: G**rade **P**oint **A**verage, the average of all grades; 4.0 is the highest GPA possible.

of a team, while SW prefers to work independently. [11]The hiring decision is difficult because both applicants are equally well qualified. [12]However, JZ would be the better choice for the receptionist job because of her experience with patient contact and preference for working with other staff. [13]If there is a future opening for a lab assistant, SW would be an excellent choice for that position.

Questions on the Models
1. Which paragraph discusses both similarities and differences?
2. Which paragraph discusses mostly differences?
3. What is the topic sentence of Paragraph 1?
4. What example does the writer give to illustrate the main point in Paragraph 1?
5. What is the topic sentence of Paragraph 2? (*Hint*: It is not the first sentence.)
6. How many similarities does the writer of Paragraph 2 describe? How many differences?

There are two ways to organize a **comparison/contrast** paragraph. One way is called block organization, and the other way is called point-by-point organization.

Block Organization

In **block organization**, you group all the similarities together in one block and all the differences together in one block. Both model paragraphs use block organization.

```
all similarities

all differences
```

Point-by-Point Organization

In **point-by-point organization**, you write about similarities and differences by subtopic. For example, if you are comparing and contrasting several wireless telephone plans, you might compare and contrast them on these subtopics:

```
cost of telephone
    (similarities and differences)

monthly rate
    (similarities and differences)

length of contract
    (similarities and differences)

reliability of service
    (similarities and differences)
```

If you have a lot to say about each subtopic, you may need to write a separate paragraph for each one.

The pattern of organization you choose depends on your topic. Also, whether you discuss more similarities or more differences (or both) depends on your topic.

A topic sentence for a comparison/contrast paragraph should name the topic and also indicate comparison/contrast organization.

> The left and right sides of your brain process information in different ways.

> When buying wireless telephone service, you should compare different plans on four points.

A concluding sentence for a comparison/contrast paragraph may repeat the main idea.

> The hiring decision is difficult because both applicants are so similar.

A concluding sentence may also make a recommendation.

> However, JX would be the better choice for the receptionist job because of her experience with patient contact and preference for working with other staff.

> In my opinion, the TeleVox telephone is the best choice for our company.

Try It Out!

Work with a partner or a small group. You are a travel agent, and a client has asked you to help her decide on a vacation destination. She wants to go during the summer, and she is considering Alaska and Hawaii. Both places are popular tourist destinations. You have gathered some information about the two places. You now need to organize this information and prepare a written report.

Step 1   Study the list of information about Alaska and Hawaii. Clarify any unfamiliar vocabulary.

Step 2   The information is not in any order. Organize the information by filling in the chart. Begin by assigning the items to one of the following main topics: accommodations, climate, or natural Beauty.

Then put the information in the appropriate boxes.

1. The quality of hotels in Alaska is quite good.
2. It often rains during the summer in Hawaii.
3. The temperature is perfect in Alaska during the summer.
4. Hawaii has Volcano National Park and Waimea Canyon.
5. Accommodations in Alaska vary from basic to luxury.
6. The beaches in Hawaii are among the most beautiful in the world.
7. The glaciers in Alaska are awesome.
8. There is a wide range of excellent hotels and condos in Hawaii, from luxury to budget priced.
9. Alaska has the Chugach Mountains and Mount McKinley, the highest mountain in North America.
10. It seldom rains during the summer in Alaska.
11. It can be hot and humid in Hawaii in the summer.
12. There is no humidity in Alaska.

Main Topics	Alaska	Hawaii
accommodations		
climate		
natural beauty	Chugach Mountains and Mount McKinley	

Step 3 Decide which pattern of organization to use in your report: block or point-by-point.

Step 4 Make an outline of your report.

Step 5 Write your report.

Sentence Structure

Just as there are signal words and phrases that help your reader understand time order, there are also words and phrases that help your reader understand similarities and differences. As you read the following model, see if you can find these comparison/contrast signals.

MODEL

*Comparison/
Contrast Signals*

Two Varieties of English

[1]Although U.S. English and British English are mutually understandable languages, there are quite a few differences. [2]One difference is spelling. [3]Some words are spelled one way in the United States but *spelt* another way in Great Britain. [4]A person goes to a British *theatre* but to a U.S. theater. [5]In U.S. schools, students theorize, analyze and socialize, whereas British students *theorise, analyse*, and *socialise*. [6]A second area of difference is vocabulary. [7]For example, the word *college* names two very different types of schools in the United States and Great Britain — university level in the United States and pre-university level in Great Britain. [8]Also, British university students live in *halls* on campus and in *flats* off campus, but U.S. students live in dormitories on campus and in apartments off campus. [9]Finally, there are many differences in pronunciation. [10]In Great Britain, the sound of *a* in the words *path, laugh, aunt, plant,* and *dance* is like the *a* in *father*. [11]In the United States, in contrast, the *a* sound in the words is like the *a* in *cat*. [12]All in all, though there are differences between the English spoken in the United States and the English spoken in the British Isles, we understand each other most of the time!

Questions on the Model
1. Underline the topic sentence. Does it indicate that the paragraph will discuss mostly similarities or mostly differences?
2. What comparison and contrast signals can you find? Circle them.
3. What other transition signals can you find? Put a box around them.
4. The model uses block organization. What pattern of organization does the writer use within the block? *Hint*: Look at the boxed transition signals.

Comparison Signals

Following is a chart of the words and phrases that show similarities. (*Note*: The numbers correspond to the numbered examples below the chart.)

Sentence Connectors	Coordinating Conjunctions	Subordinating Conjunctions	Others	Paired Conjunctions

1. similarly
   likewise
1a. also
1b. too
	2. and . . . (too)	**3.** as
		   just as
			4. similar
			   equal
			   the same
			4a. similar to
			   equal to
			   (just) like
			   the same as
			4b. equally
				5. both . . . and
				   not only . . . but also

1. Sentence connectors can appear in various places in a sentence. *(See page 84 to review their use.)*

   Tokyo is the financial heart of Japan. **Similarly/Likewise,** New York is the center of banking and finance in the United States.

1a. *Also* often appears in the middle or at the end of a sentence. Don't use *also* with a semicolon.

   Tokyo is a major financial center. New York is a center of banking and finance **also.**

   Tokyo is the financial heart of Japan. New York is **also** a center of banking and finance.

1b. and 2. *Too* usually comes at the end of a sentence. It often appears together with the coordinating conjunction *and*. Some writers put a comma before *too* at the end of a sentence, but it is not required.

   Tokyo is a center of style and fashion; New York is, **too.**

   Tokyo is a center of style and fashion, **and** New York is **too.**

3. *As* is a subordinating word. It begins a dependent clause. The word *just* makes it stronger. Notice that you use a comma even when the independent clause comes first. This is an exception to the usual rule.

   Tokyo is trendy and hip, **as/just as** New York is.

4. These words act like adjectives; that is, they describe nouns.

   Tokyo's and New York's traffic problems are **similar/equal/the same.**

   Tokyo and New York have **similar/equal/the same** traffic problems.

4a. These words act like prepositions. They come in front of nouns.

   Tokyo's traffic is **similar to/(just) like/the same as** New York's.

   Like New York, Tokyo has traffic problems.

4b. *Equally* is an adverb. It describes an adjective (*crowded*). An adverb can also describe a verb or another adverb.

> Tokyo and New York City are **equally** crowded.

5. Paired conjunctions are always used together. Notice that the word that comes after the second conjunction must be the same part of speech (noun, verb, prepositional phrase, etc.) as the word that comes after the first conjunction. This is an important rule in English and is called the rule of **parallelism**.

> The two cities are **both** trendy **and** hip.
>
> The two cities are **not only** trendy **but also** hip.

RIGHT

> The two cities are both **trendy** *(adjective)* and **hip.** *(adjective)*

WRONG

> The two cities are both **noisy** *(adjective)* and **have too many people.** *(verb phrase)*

> Both **New York City** and **Tokyo** have outstanding international restaurants. *(nouns)*
>
> Tokyoites and New Yorkers can both **eat** and **drink** in any kind of restaurant. *(verbs)*
>
> The two cities have both **positive** and **negative** features. *(adjectives)*
>
> Not only **Tokyoites** but also **New Yorkers** dress fashionably. *(nouns)*
>
> You can see joggers not only **in Central Park** but also **in Hibuya Park.** *(prepositional phrases)*

PRACTICE 1

Comparison Signals

A. Circle all the comparison signals in the model paragraph "Miller Medical Labs Memorandum" on page 110.

B. Complete the following sentences. Be sure to follow the rule of parallelism.

1. Both in Tokyo and ____in New York City____ the art museums display many famous masterpieces.

2. Both overcrowded subways and _____ are problems in Tokyo and New York City.

3. You can buy designer clothes not only in boutiques but also _____ .

4. New Yorkers and Tokyoites can not only see a movie but can also _____ at any time.

5. In the summer, the weather in Tokyo and in New York is both hot and _____ .

6. The Ginza and Fifth Avenue shopping districts have both fine jewelry stores and _____ .

C. Combine the ideas in the two sentences, using the comparison structure word in parentheses. Punctuate your new sentences carefully.

1. Magazine and newspaper advertising information about new products to the public. Radio, television, and Internet ads tell the public what's new. (similarly)

   <u>Magazine and newspaper advertising information about a product to the public.</u>

   <u>Similarly, radio, television, and Internet ads tell the public what's new.</u>

2. Newspapers and magazines need advertising to pay their costs. Radio and television need advertising to pay their costs. (like)

   _____

   _____

3. The media[1] reach millions of people around the world. The Internet reaches people everywhere. (similarly)

   _____

   _____

4. Most people read a daily newspaper. Most people listen to the radio or watch television every day. (just as)

   _____

   _____

5. Printed pictures are powerful advertising media. Video pictures are powerful advertising media. (equally)

   _____

   _____

D. Write sentences of comparison using the words and phrases given. In all sentences, you will have to supply a verb.

1. The Spanish language/the Italian language (similar to)

   <u>The Spanish language is similar to the Italian language.</u>

   _____

2. Knowing a second language/useful/travel/employment (not only . . . but also)

   _____

   _____

(continued on next page)

---

[1]**the media:** newspapers, magazines, radio, television, and so on. *Media* is a plural noun. The singular form is *medium.*

3. Male students/female students/school sports/participate in (like)

_____

_____

4. High school students going to college/high school students not going to college/graduation requirements. (the same . . . as)

_____

_____

5. Private/public universities/good education (both . . . and)

_____

_____

Contrast Signals

Contrast signals point out differences.

Sentence Connectors	Coordinating Conjunctions	Subordinating Conjunctions	Others
1. in contrast on the other hand however	2. but 2a. yet	3. while whereas 3a. although even though though	4. different(ly) from unlike 5. differ (from) (in)

1. Sentence connectors connect two independent clauses.

   Most baby animals can walk within a few hours of birth. **In contrast/On the other hand/However,** a human baby needs about 12 months to learn this skill.

2. Use *but* when the ideas are exact opposites.

   The language center is on the left side of the brains of right-handed people, **but** it is on the right side of left-handed and ambidextrous[1] people.

2a. Use *yet* when one idea is a surprising or unexpected continuation of the other idea. It is also possible to use *but*.

   The left side of the brain controls logic and reasoning, **yet** it also controls language.

_____

[1]**ambidextrous:** able to use both hands equally

3. Use *while* and *whereas* when the ideas are exact opposites. *While* and *whereas* can begin either clause. Always use a comma even when the independent clause comes first. This is an exception to the usual rule.

> I have brown eyes, **while/whereas** my brother's eyes are green.

> **While/whereas** I have brown eyes, my brother's eyes are green.

3a. Use *although*, *even though*, or *though* when one idea is a surprising or unexpected continuation of the other idea. *Although*, *even though*, and *though* can sometimes (but not always) begin either clause.

> My grandfather is the wisest man in our town **although/even though/though** he never finished high school.

> **Although/even though/though** he never finished high school, my grandfather is the wisest man in our town.

4. *From* and *unlike* are both prepositions. Put a noun or noun phrase after them. *Differently* is an adverb. It describes the verbs *think* and *learn*.

> The way left-brained people think and learn is **different from** the way right-brained people do.

> **Unlike** left-brainers, right-brainers often know the answer to a math problem without knowing how they got it.

> Left-brained people think and learn **differently from** the way right-brained people do.

5. *Differ* is a verb.

> Left-brain and right-brain people **differ** in the way they think and learn.

PRACTICE 2
Contrast Signals

A. Circle the words that show contrast in the model paragraph "Right Brain/Left Brain" on page 109.

B. Write contrast sentences using the given information. Use a coordinating conjunction, a subordinating conjunction, and a sentence connector.

1. Mary likes to go out at night. Jin prefers quiet evenings at home.

   a. Mary likes to go out at night, but Jin prefers quiet evenings at home.

   b. Mary likes to go out at night, whereas Jin prefers quiet evenings at home.

   c. Mary likes to go out at night. However, Jin prefers quiet evenings at home.

2. Fresh fruits and vegetables taste delicious. Canned ones are tasteless.

   a. _____

   b. _____

   c. _____

(continued on next page)

3. Eating well and exercising will keep you in good health. Exercising by itself will not.

    a. _____

    b. _____

    c. _____

4. A university has a graduate school. A college usually does not.

    a. _____

    b. _____

    c. _____

5. Marco will go to college on a full scholarship. Peter will have to work part time.

    a. _____

    b. _____

    c. _____

6. Medical care is free in Canada. People must pay for it in the United States.

    a. _____

    b. _____

    c. _____

C. Complete the sentences of comparison or contrast with the signal words and phrases in parentheses.

1. (but) In the United States, people drive on the right side of a road,

    but in other countries, they drive on the left. _____

2. (yet) Professor Rand's first exam was easy _____

    _____

3. (although) Texting is a popular new way to communicate _____

    _____

4. (whereas) _____

    _____ my grandparents do not know how to turn a computer on.

5. (different from) The method of cooking rice in China_____

    _____

Review

These are the important points covered in this chapter:

1. A comparison/contrast paragraph explains what is similar and/or different about two (or more) things.

2. In block organization, you discuss all the similarities together and all the differences together.

3. In point-by-point organization, you discuss subtopics in any order.

4. The topic sentence should name the topic and also indicate comparison and contrast organization. The concluding sentence can repeat the main idea and make a recommendation.

5. Use comparison and contrast signals to show similarities and differences.

Skill Sharpeners

The following exercises will help you review important skills you learned in prior chapters.

EXERCISE 1
Outlining

Practice your outlining skills. On a separate piece of paper, make a detailed outline of the model paragraph "Two Varieties of English" on page 114.

EXERCISE 2
Summary Writing

Practice your summarizing skills. On a separate piece of paper, write a summary of each of the three model paragraphs in this chapter. Remember that a summary includes only the main points and none of the details. Try to summarize the models "Right Brain/Left Brain" on page 109 and "Miller Medical Labs Memorandum" on page 110 in five or fewer sentences. Try to summarize the model "Two Varieties of English" on page 114 in two sentences.

Writing Assignment

Write a paragraph comparing and contrasting two school systems.

Follow these five steps:

Step 1 Interview someone who is not from your culture or country about elementary and/or secondary educational systems. Choose *one* subtopic ("time spent in school" *or* "curriculum[1]" *or* "teachers and teaching styles" *or* "other") and fill in the appropriate section of the chart. Then write a paragraph telling about the similarities and differences you discovered.

Step 2 Organize the ideas by making an outline.

- Decide whether to organize your topic in a block pattern or in a point-by-point pattern.
- Write a topic sentence that indicates a comparison/contrast type of paragraph.

Step 3 Write the rough draft. Write ROUGH DRAFT at the top of your paper.

- Focus on using comparison and contrast signals appropriately.

Step 4 Polish the rough draft.

- Exchange papers with a classmate and ask him or her to check your rough draft using Peer-Editing Worksheet 7 on page 210. Then discuss the completed worksheet and decide what changes you should make. Write a second draft.
- Use Self-Editing Worksheet 7 on page 211 to check your second draft for grammar, punctuation, and sentence structure.

Step 5 Write a final copy. Hand in your rough draft, your second draft, your final copy, and the page containing the two editing worksheets. Your teacher may also ask you to hand in your prewriting paper.

Caution! Limit your paragraph to one subtopic; otherwise, your paragraph will not have unity.

---

[1]**curriculum:** courses of study

Systems of Education

	My Country: _____	Other Country: _____
Subtopic 1	**Time Spent in School**	
How many years are students required to attend school?		
How are these years divided?		
How many hours per day are students at school? How many days per week?		
How many weeks of vacation are there? When are the vacations?		
Subtopic 2	**Curriculum**	
What academic subjects do students study in elementary school? In high school? What nonacademic subjects do they take (music, art, etc.)?		
How many hours of homework do students have each night or each week?		
Is there a different teacher for each subject?		
Do students have to take exams to pass into the next grade? When do they take exams?		

(continued on next page)

Systems of Education *(continued)*

Subtopic 3	Teachers and Teaching Styles	
Are the teachers mostly men or women?		
What kind of training do teachers have?		
Is the classroom atmosphere formal or informal? Do students stand up when teachers enter the room? How do students behave? Do students sit at desks or at tables? How are they arranged in the room?		
How do teachers grade students? How do teachers reward or punish students?		
Do students discuss and ask questions, or do they just listen and answer questions asked by the teacher?		
Subtopic 4	Other	
Do students wear uniforms?		
What extracurricular activities are there at school (clubs, sports teams, school plays, etc.)?		
Are parents active in the schools? How do parents participate?		
(Ask some questions of your own.)		

Alternative Writing Topics

Compare or contrast two cultures on these topics:

meals and meal times	parents' roles
foods eaten for breakfast	ways of raising children
driving habits	courtship customs

Other topic suggestions:

climate in two regions	punctual people/tardy people
homes in two regions	neat people/messy people
two restaurants in your area	shopping habits of men and women
morning people/night people	dogs and cats as pets

Definition Paragraphs

Organization

Sentence Structure

Appositives

Adjective Clauses

Complex Sentences with Adjective Clauses

Subject Pronouns: *who*, *which*, and *that*

Object Pronouns: *whom*, *which*, *that*, and Ø (no pronoun)

Clauses with *when*

Review

Writing Assignment

Organization

People who are interested in your culture may ask you to explain a word that they have heard but do not understand, such as Spanish *machismo* or German *Gemütlichkeit*, or an interesting custom or practice such as *casual Friday* or *Saint Patrick's Day* in the United States, *O-bon* festivals in Japan, *holi* festivals in India, or *quinceañera* parties in Spanish-influenced cultures.

Tests of general writing ability sometimes ask you to define abstract[1] terms such as *love*, *friendship*, *courage*, or *happiness*. Tests in college classes may contain questions such as these:

LAW ENFORCEMENT   What are Miranda rights?

LANDSCAPE DESIGN   What are organic soil amendments, and how do they improve soil?

U.S. HISTORY   What was the Underground Railroad?

HEALTH SCIENCES   What is the Rh factor, and why is it important to pregnant women and their babies?

These kinds of questions ask you to define or explain something; for our purposes, we will simply call them *definition paragraphs*.

MODELS
Definition Paragraphs

Paragraph 1

The Underground Railroad[2]

[1]The Underground Railroad was a secret system that helped slaves escape from slavery in the United States during the mid-1800s. [2]It was not a real railroad; rather, it was a loosely organized chain of people and safe houses[3] that stretched from the slave states of the South to the free states of the North and Canada. [3]The escapees traveled mostly on foot at night and hid during the day. [4]Free blacks and some whites helped the escapees, giving them food, clothing, places to hide, and directions to the next safe house. [5]Indeed, the Underground Railroad was a remarkable system that helped thousands of slaves find safety and freedom.

[1]**abstract:** cannot be touched or seen; exists only in a person's mind
[2]The picture on page 125 shows slaves escaping to freedom on the Underground Railroad.
[3]**safe houses:** houses where people can hide when their enemies are looking for them

Paragraph 2

Courage

¹Courage is the quality of being brave when you are facing something that is dangerous or that you fear. ²For example, a soldier who goes into battle shows courage. ³A paramedic⁴ who crawls into a collapsed building to help an injured person also shows courage. ⁴However, you don't have to be a soldier or a paramedic to be courageous. ⁵You can display courage in everyday situations, too. ⁶For instance, a shy person who is afraid of speaking in public shows courage when he or she gives a speech at school or at work. ⁷A teenager who resists peer pressure to smoke, drink, or try drugs shows courage. ⁸To give another example, my friend Angela, who is terrified of flying, recently took her first airplane flight. ⁹As she walked onto the plane, she was trembling with fear, but she didn't give in to her fright. ¹⁰To me, Angela entering that airplane was as brave as a soldier entering battle.

Questions on the Models
1. In each model paragraph, identify the three parts of the topic sentence: topic, category or group, distinguishing characteristics. (Read the information and chart below first.)
2. Which paragraph uses examples in the supporting sentences?
3. Which paragraph uses facts to answer *who*, *what*, *where*, *why*, *when*, and *how* questions?

One way to write the topic sentence of a definition paragraph is to give three pieces of information:

1. The word or thing you will define or explain (the topic)
2. The large category or group to which the word or thing belongs
3. The distinguishing characteristics that make it different from other members of the category

Term/Person/Concept	Category or Group	Distinguishing Characteristics
The Underground Railroad was . . .	a secret system . . .	that helped slaves escape from the South to freedom in the North during the mid-1800s.
Courage is . . .	the quality . . .	of being brave when you are facing something that is dangerous or that you fear.
Casual Friday refers to . . .	the custom . . .	of office workers wearing casual clothes to work on Fridays.

⁴**paramedic:** a person who is trained to give emergency medical help

In the supporting sentences, add details that explain the topic more completely. The supporting sentences may give additional facts telling *who*, *what*, *where*, *when*, *how*, or *why*, an explanation of a process, examples, or a description.

In the concluding sentence, you may tell why the topic is important, interesting, or unique.

PRACTICE 1

Topic Sentences for Definition Paragraphs

Complete each topic sentence for a definition paragraph with (1) a category or group and (2) distinguishing characteristics. Use a dictionary if necessary.

1. A dictator is _____a ruler_____ who _____has all the power in a country_____ .

2. An optimist is _____ who _____ .

3. A good friend is _____ who _____ .

4. An ideal spouse is _____ who _____ .

5. Chess is _____ that _____ .

Try It Out!

Choose four words of your own to define in topic sentences for definition paragraphs. *Note*: You may want to use one of these topics for your own paragraph at the end of the chapter.

Ask your classmates or your teacher if there is anything they want to know about your country or your culture. Think of words or things that someone outside your age group or your cultural group might not understand. Examples:

> *ikebana* and *bonsai* (Japan)
> *la passeggiata* (Italy)
> *Día de los Muertos* and *Las Posadas* (Mexico)
> Groundhog Day and Sadie Hawkins Day (United States)
> *Stammtisch* (Germany)
> *samovar* (Russia, other countries)

Sentence Structure

In this section, you will learn to write appositives and adjective clauses. Appositives are nouns that rename other nouns, and adjective clauses are another kind of dependent clause. The ability to use appositives and adjective clauses is the mark of mature writing style.

As you read the model paragraph, look for sentences that contain the words *who*, *which*, and *that*. Underline the clauses that begin with these words.

Holidays with Pagan[1] Origins

[1] Many cultures have holidays that have pagan origins. [2] *No Rooz*, Iranian New Year, which begins on the first day of spring, is one of these. [3] Iranians

celebrate the passing of the old year with bonfires and the entrance of the new year with special foods. [4] On a special table, they display seven foods with names that start with the letter *s* in Farsi, the language of Iran. [5] The seven foods represent life, health, wealth, abundance, love, patience, and purity. [6] Other objects representing a good year are put on the table: a mirror, candles, eggs, and a goldfish. [7] Another example of a holiday with pagan origins is Halloween, which is celebrated in the United States on October 31. [8] On Halloween night, children dress up in costumes and go from house to house to get candy. [9] The children dress up as witches, ghosts, black cats, princesses, cowboys, Spiderman, Wonder Woman, or a favorite animal. [10] People also carve frightening faces in pumpkins and put candles inside them at night. [11] All these customs started hundreds of years ago in Ireland and England. [12] There people celebrated the end of the farming season by lighting bonfires, large outdoor fires, to keep away bad spirits that might appear in the night. [13] The ancient Irish and English people also dressed up as ghosts to frighten away bad spirits. [14] From these examples, we can see that many holidays are not "holy[2] days" at all; rather, they developed from pagan celebrations.

---

[1] **pagan:** not religious
[2] **holy:** religious

Appositives

Appositives are nouns or noun phrases that rename a preceding noun or noun phrase.

1. They set up a special table on which they display seven foods with names beginning with the letter *s* in Farsi, **the language of Iran**.

2. There people celebrated the end of the farming season by lighting bonfires, **large outdoor fires**, to keep away bad spirits who might appear in the night.

In sentence 1, *Farsi* and *the language of Iran* are the same thing. In sentence 2, *bonfires* and *large outdoor fires* are the same thing. *The language of Iran* and *large outdoor fires* are appositives.

Appositives are very useful in writing definitions because they give the reader more information about your topic concisely (without a lot of extra words).

> Fudge, **a delicious chocolate candy,** was invented as a result of a cooking mistake.

Appositives can be necessary information or extra information.[1] Consider this sentence:

> My friend **Tim** got married last week.

In this sentence, *Tim* is an appositive because *Tim* and *my friend* are the same person. *Tim* is a necessary appositive because it is necessary to identify which friend got married. If we omit the word *Tim*, we don't know which friend got married.

Now consider this sentence:

> Tim, **my friend**, got married last week.

In this sentence, the appositive is *my friend*. It is extra information because the name *Tim* already identifies the person who got married. If we omit *my friend*, we still know who got married. The fact that he is the writer's friend is not necessary to identify him. It is merely extra information.

If there is only one of an item, it is unnecessary to identify it further, so appositives of one-of-a-kind items are always extra information. For example, Earth has only one moon, so any appositive of *the Moon* in a sentence would be extra information. Similarly, adjectives such as *tallest*, *strongest*, *oldest*, and *most interesting* automatically make the following noun one of a kind.

> The Moon, **Earth's only natural satellite**, orbits Earth about once a month.

> The highest mountain in North America, **Mount McKinley**, is in Alaska.

The appositive *Mount McKinley* is extra information because it follows *the highest*, and there can be only one "highest."

> I have three sons. My son **Carlos** looks like me.

Carlos is necessary information because there are three sons, and the name *Carlos* is necessary to identify which son.

---

[1]**necessary information** or **extra information:** Most grammar books use the terms *restrictive* or *nonrestrictive*.

My youngest son, **Javier**, looks like his father.

The appositive *Javier* is extra information because there can be only one youngest son.

Comma Rule

Use commas to separate an extra information appositive from the rest of the sentence. Do not use commas with necessary appositives.

PRACTICE 2

Commas with Appositives

A. Locate and underline as many appositives as you can find in the model paragraph on page 129. Explain the use of commas in each one.

B. Identify and punctuate appositives.

Step 1 Underline the appositive in each of the following sentences.

Step 2 Decide whether it is necessary or extra information, and write NI for *necessary information* or EI for *extra information* on the line.

Step 3 Add commas around unnecessary appositives.

__NI__ 1. The planet <u>Pluto</u> is more than 2.5 billion miles from Earth.

__EI__ 2. Pluto, <u>the most distant planet from Earth</u>, is more than 2.5 billion miles away.

_____ 3. Venus the closest planet to Earth is only 25 million miles away.

_____ 4. The largest planet in the universe Jupiter is eleven times larger than Earth.

_____ 5. Astronomers scientists who study the stars discovered a tenth planet in our solar system in 2005.

_____ 6. The Moon is Earth's only natural satellite, but the planet Saturn has at least twenty-two satellites.

_____ 7. Since the first artificial satellite Sputnik 1 was launched by Russia in 1957, thousands of space probes, satellites, and telescopes have been sent into space.

_____ 8. Also, millions of pieces of space junk man-made garbage zoom around Earth at speeds of up to 25,000 miles per hour.

Adjective Clauses

Adjective clauses are dependent clauses. They are called adjective clauses because, like adjectives, they modify nouns and pronouns. They begin with the words *who*, *whom*, *which*, and *that*, among others. These words are called *relative pronouns*, and adjective clauses are also called *relative clauses*. An adjective clause joined to an independent clause makes a complex sentence.

Because we use adjective clauses to give more information about a noun, they are very useful in writing definitions.

> Propaganda is a form of communication **that tries to influence people's thinking and actions.**

> Latino music, **which has many different styles and artists,** is becoming increasingly popular in the United States.

> Sadie Hawkins' Day is a day **when women can invite men to dance or to go out on a date.**

Like appositives, adjectives clauses can be necessary or extra information. Use the same comma rule.

Comma Rule

Use commas to separate an extra information adjective clause from the rest of the sentence. Do not use commas with necessary adjective clauses.

NECESSARY
> Every culture in the world has special days **that people observe with traditional food, customs, and events.**

In this sentence, the clause *that people observe with traditional food, customs, and events* is an adjective clause modifying the noun *days*. Since it is necessary to identify which days the writer is discussing, the clause is necessary and commas are not used. *That* always introduces a necessary clause.

EXTRA INFORMATION
> Another example of a modern holiday with pagan origins is Halloween, **which is on October 31.**

In this sentence, the clause *which is on October 31* is an adjective clause modifying the noun *Halloween*. The clause is unnecessary to identify *Halloween*; it merely gives extra information about it. Therefore, commas are used. *Which*, *who*, and *whom* introduce extra information clauses.

PRACTICE 3

Commas with Adjective Clauses

Identify and punctuate adjective clauses.

Step 1 Underline the adjective clauses in the following sentences.

Step 2 Draw an arrow to the noun each one modifies.

Step 3 Decide whether each one is necessary information or extra information, and write NI or EI on the line.

Step 4 Add commas if they are needed.

Easter

   EI   1. Some of the customs of Easter, <u>which is a Christian holiday</u>, have pagan origins.

_____ 2. Before Christianity existed, people in northern and central Europe worshipped a goddess whom they called Eostre.

_____ 3. Eostre which means *east* was the goddess of spring.

_____ 4. Every spring, people who worshipped her held a festival to give thanks for the return of the sun's warmth.

_____ 5. They offered the goddess cakes that they baked for the festival.

_____ 6. These cakes were very similar to hot cross buns which bakeries sell at Easter.

_____ 7. Also, the custom of coloring eggs which families do at Easter came from ancient cultures.

_____ 8. Even the popular Easter bunny who brings chocolate eggs and other candy to children on Easter Sunday has pagan roots.

Complex Sentences with Adjective Clauses

We make sentences with adjective clauses by combining two sentences.

> Easter is named for a pagan goddess. + Easter is a Christian holiday.

> ADJECTIVE CLAUSE
> Easter, **which is a Christian holiday,** is named for a pagan goddess.

The clause *which is a Christian holiday* is an adjective clause that modifies the noun *Easter*. The modified noun is called the **antecedent**.

Here are some important points about adjective clauses.

1. Place an adjective clause after its antecedent and as close to it as possible to avoid confusion.

CONFUSING   He left the car on the street that he had just bought. *(Did he buy a car or a street?)*

CLEAR   He left the car that he had just bought on the street.

2. When a relative pronoun is the subject of the adjective clause, make the verb in the clause agree with its antecedent.

> ANTECEDENT   S   V
> **A teacher** who **teaches** young children needs a lot of patience.
> ANTECEDENT   S   V
> **Teachers** who **teach** young children need a lot of patience.

3. Don't use double pronouns.

> Last night we watched reruns of *Friends*, which ̶i̶t̶ is my favorite TV show.

4. When you make an adjective clause, choose an appropriate relative pronoun.

Subject Pronouns: *who*, *which*, and *that*

When a relative pronoun is the subject of an adjective clause, choose a subject pronoun: *who*, *which*, or *that*.

	People	**Things**
Extra Information	**who**	**which**
Necessary Information	**who** **that** (informal)	**which** **that**

- *Who* is used for people.
- *Which* is used for things.
- *That* is used for people and things. Using *that* for people is informal.
- Use *that* in necessary clauses only.

Extra Information

The Nobel Prizes are named for Alfred Nobel. + **He** was a citizen of Sweden.

The Nobel Prizes are named for Alfred Nobel, **who** was a citizen of Sweden.

April Fool's Day is a day for playing tricks on your friends. + **It** is on April 1.

April Fool's Day, **which** is on April 1, is a day for playing tricks on your friends.

Necessary Information

The student is from Thailand. + **She** got the best score on the last test.

The student **who** got the best score on the last test is from Thailand.

The student **that** got the best score on the last test is from Thailand.

Leap Day is a special day. + **It** happens only every four years.

Leap Day is a special day **which** happens only every four years.

Leap Day is a special day **that** happens only every four years.

PRACTICE 4

Adjective Clauses with Subject Pronouns

A. Make an adjective clause from the sentence in parentheses in each of the following pairs. Write it on the line to make a complex sentence. Add commas if they are needed.

1. Many religions have rules about food <u>that were developed for health reasons</u>. (The rules were developed for health reasons.)

2. Judaism _____ has very strict rules about food. (Judaism is the oldest major religion in the world.)

3. Christians _____ do not eat certain foods during the six weeks before Easter. (Some Christians practice fasting.)

4. People _____ cannot eat beef. (People practice the Hindu religion.)

5. Muslims and Jews cannot eat pork _____. (Pork is considered unclean.)

6. Muslims cannot eat or drink at all in the daytime during Ramadan _____ _____. (Ramadan is a holy month of fasting.)

B. Combine the sentences in each of the following pairs by making one of them an adjective clause and joining it to the other sentence. Be careful to put the clause immediately after the noun it modifies. Add commas if they are needed.

1. Three of the world's major religions were started by men. The men were teachers.

   <u>Three of the world's major religions were started by men who were teachers</u>.

2. Gautama Siddhartha was born about 500 years before Jesus. Gautama Siddhartha started Buddhism.

   _____

3. Christianity was started by Jesus. Jesus was born about 500 years before Mohammed.

   _____

4. Mohammed founded Islam. Islam is the second largest religion in the word.

   _____

5. A religion is monotheistic. A religion has one God.

   _____

6. The Hindu and Shinto religions are polytheistic. The Hindu and Shinto religions have many gods.

   _____

Object Pronouns: *whom, which, that,* and Ø (no pronoun)

When the relative pronoun is an object in an adjective clause, choose the object pronoun *whom*, *which*, or *that*, or use no pronoun.

	People	**Things**
Extra Information	**whom**	**which**
Necessary Information	**whom** **that** (informal) Ø	**which** **that** Ø

- *Whom* is used for people. Informally, *who* is used instead of *whom*.
- *Which* is used for things.
- *That* is used for people and things. Using *that* for people is informal.
- Use *that* in necessary clauses only.
- You may omit an object relative pronoun in necessary clauses only.
- Notice that an object pronoun is placed at the beginning of the adjective clause, before the subject.

Extra Information

Professor Lee is my chemistry teacher. We saw **him** at the supermarket.

Professor Lee, **whom** we saw at the supermarket, is my chemistry teacher.

Boxing Day is unknown in the United States. People in Canada, Great Britain, and many other English-speaking countries celebrate **Boxing Day**.

Boxing Day, **which** people in Canada, Great Britain, and many other English-speaking countries celebrate, is unknown in the United States.

Necessary

The person is my teacher. We saw **her** at the supermarket.

The person **whom** we saw at the supermarket is my chemistry teacher.

The person **that** we saw at the supermarket is my chemistry teacher.

The person we saw at the supermarket is my chemistry teacher.

The film was long. We saw **it** last week.

The film **which** we saw last week was long.

The film **that** we saw last week was long.

The film we saw last week was long.

PRACTICE 5

Adjective Clauses with Object Pronouns

A. Make an adjective clause from the sentence in parentheses in each of the following pairs. Write it on the line to make a complex sentence. Add commas if they are needed.

1. People in Thailand have a festival _____

_____.

(They call the festival *Loy Krathong,* "Festival of the Floating Leaf Cups.")

2. The Thais float little boats _____

_____

down a river in the evening. (They have made the little boats out of banana leaves, lotus, or paper.)

    3. The boats _____

    _____

    float down the river in the moonlight. (They have decorated the boats with lighted candles, incense, coins, and flowers.)

B. Combine the sentences in each of the following pairs by making one of them an adjective clause and joining it to the other sentence. Be careful to put the clause immediately after the noun it modifies. Add commas if they are needed.

Pongal is a three-day festival that celebrates the rice harvest in southern India.

    1. On the first day of *Pongal,* families gather in the kitchen and boil a pot of new rice. They cook the new rice in milk.

    _____

    _____

    2. Then they offer some of the sweet rice to the sun god. They thank the sun god for ripening the rice crop. (Use *whom.*)

    _____

    _____

    3. The second day of *Pongal* is for the rain. They thank the rain for helping the rice to grow. (Use *which.*)

    _____

    _____

    4. A traditional *Pongal* gift is a clay horse. They paint the horse in bright colors.

    _____

    _____

    5. On the third day of *Pongal,* the farmers honor their cattle. They decorate the cattle with flowers and coins.

    _____

    _____

Clauses with *when*

You can begin a clause with *when* to give more information about a time.

	Time
Extra Information	**when**
Necessary Information	**when**

- *When* replaces a prepositional phrase or the word *then.*
- *When* can begin both extra and necessary-information clauses.

Extra Information

A popular day with children is Halloween. They dress up in costumes and get

candy from neighbors <u>on Halloween</u>.

PREP. PHRASE

A popular day with children is Halloween, **when** they dress up in costumes and get candy from neighbors.

Necessary Information

Ramadan is a time. + Muslims fast <u>then</u>.

Ramadan is a time **when** Muslims fast.

PRACTICE 6 *Clauses with* When	Combine the sentences in each of the following pairs by making one of them a clause beginning with *when* and joining it to the other sentence. Be careful to put the clause immediately after the noun it modifies. Add commas if they are needed.

1. Were you alive on July 20, 1969? The first human walked on the moon on that day.

   _____

2. Every mother remembers the wonderful day. Her first child was born on that day.

   _____

3. *Tet* is a special time. Vietnamese people celebrate the lunar new year then.

   _____

The following chart summarizes important information about adjective clauses:

Review Chart: Adjective Clauses

To refer to people				
who	refers to people	subject in its own clause	necessary information OR extra information	The student **who gave the best speech** won a prize. Kim Leong, **who gave the best speech,** won a prize.
whom	refers to people	object in its own clause	necessary information OR extra information	She loaned her car to someone **whom she did not know.** She loaned her car to Tom, **whom she has known for a long time.**

To refer to animals and things				
which	refers to animals and things	subject or object in its own clause	extra information only	She teaches biology, **which is my favorite subject**. Her husband teaches algebra, **which I enjoy the least**.
that	refers to animals and things; informally, refers to people	subject or object in its own clause; if *that* is an object, it may be omitted	necessary information only	The class **that meets in the next room** is very noisy. The subject **that I enjoy the least** is algebra. The subject **I enjoy the least** is algebra. The salesman **that sold me my car** was fired. (informal)
To refer to time				
when	refers to a time		necessary information OR extra information	I work full time on days **when I do not have classes**. I did not work at all last week, **when I had my final exams**.

PRACTICE 7

Adjective Clauses

A. Write sentences with adjective clauses on your own. Define each of the following words with a sentence that contains an adjective clause. Use the words in parentheses to build your definition. Look up the words you don't know in a dictionary. All your sentences will be necessary.

1. fortune teller (a person) A fortune teller is a person who can see into the future.

_____

2. coach (a person) _____

_____

3. travel agents (people) _____

_____

4. MP3 players (devices) _____

_____

5. fork (a utensil) _____

_____

6. chopsticks (utensils) _____

_____

7. (day/time) _____

_____

(Write in a special day or period of several days in your culture.)

(continued on next page)

B. From the following list of English slang words and phrases, choose five and write definitions for them. Your definition should include at least one complex sentence containing an adjective clause. Look in a dictionary or ask a native English speaker if you need help.

blog	nutcase	slam dunk
airhead	potluck dinner	dot com
couch potato	sitting duck	tightwad
no-brainer	geek	emoticon

1. _____

_____

2. _____

_____

3. _____

_____

4. _____

_____

5. _____

_____

Try It Out!

Combine the sentences in each group in any logical way to make one sentence. Your final sentence may be simple, compound, or complex. Look for opportunities to make adjective clauses. You may add words, delete words, or change words, but you must not omit any information or change the meaning. Write your final copy as a paragraph on a separate piece of paper.

The First Thanksgiving

1. An important family holiday in the United States is Thanksgiving. It celebrates the successful harvest of some of the first European settlers in North America.

   An important holiday in the United States is Thanksgiving, which celebrates the successful harvest of some of the first European settlers in North America.

2. A modern Thanksgiving is similar in many ways to the first Thanksgiving. The first Thanksgiving took place almost four hundred years ago. It took place in the English colony of Massachusetts.

3. In 1620, the Pilgrims arrived in Plymouth, Massachusetts.
   The Pilgrims were a religious group from England.

4. The Pilgrims came to the New World.
   Their religion was different from the main religion in England.
   (Use *because*.)

5. The Pilgrims' first winter was very hard.
   Almost half the group died.

6. They died of hunger.
   They died of cold.
   They died of disease.

7. The Wampanoag helped them.
   The Wampanoag were a tribe of Native Americans in Massachusetts.
   They did this during the next year.
   (Put the time expression first.)

8. The Wampanoag taught the newcomers how to hunt.
   The Wampanoag taught the newcomers how to grow corn.
   The Wampanoag taught the newcomers how to survive in the New World.

9. The next winter came.
   The Pilgrims had enough food.

10. They were grateful.
    They had a feast to give thanks.

11. They shared food with the Wampanoag
    They shared friendship with the Wampanoag.
    They invited the Wampanoag to the feast.
    (Use *whom*.)

12. A modern Thanksgiving is similar in spirit to the first Thanksgiving.
    The food is probably different.

13. Today Americans eat turkey.
    The Pilgrims and Wampanoag probably ate deer.

Review

These are the important points covered in this chapter:

1. A definition paragraph explains the meaning and significance of something.
   The topic sentence of a definition paragraph gives three pieces of information:
   (1) the topic, (2) the large category or group, and (3) the distinguishing
   characteristics.

2. An appositive is a noun (or noun phrase) that renames another noun (or noun phrase). Appositives can be either necessary information (restrictive) or extra information (nonrestrictive). Extra-information appositives are separated from the rest of the sentence by commas.

3. An adjective clause is a dependent clause that modifies (tells more about) a noun or pronoun.

   - Adjective clauses follow the noun or pronoun they modify.
   - Adjective clauses begin with the words *who*, *whom*, *which*, and *that*, among others. These words are called relative pronouns.
   - Use *who*, *which*, and *that* when the relative pronoun is the subject of its clause.
   - Use *whom*, *which*, *that*, or no pronoun when the relative pronoun is an object in its clause.
   - Adjective clauses are either necessary information or extra information. Use commas around information clauses.

Skill Sharpeners

The following exercises will help you review important skills you learned in prior chapters.

EXERCISE 1

Scrambled Definition Paragraph

A. On a separate piece of paper, write the following sentences in the correct order to make a definition paragraph.

B. Find and underline three adjective clauses and one appositive.

Walter Gropius

1. Another major contribution to the building industry was his promotion of designs that could be mass-produced.

2. In contrast to the ornately decorated stone structures of an earlier era, Gropius's steel and glass buildings had straight lines and no ornamentation.

3. Gropius was also known for his belief in the value of teamwork, and he worked together with other architects on many projects.

4. He was influential mainly when he was the director of Germany's Bauhaus school of design.

5. In sum, Gropius and his followers transformed cities from Toronto to Tokyo.

6. Walter Gropius was a German-born architect who designed simple "glass box" buildings and changed the look of cities worldwide.

7. At the Bauhaus, Gropius was a leader of the International Style of the 1920s, a style that greatly changed building design.

EXERCISE 2
Unity

Cross out one sentence that breaks the unity of the paragraph.

Kimchi

[1]Kimchi, or kimchee, is Korea's national dish. [2]It is made of fermented[1] vegetables. [3]There are many ways to make kimchi, but it usually contains Chinese cabbage, salt, garlic, red pepper, green onion, fish sauce, and ginger. [4]These ingredients are mixed together, put into a container, and allowed to ferment for three or four days. [5]Nutritionists say that kimchi is very good for you. [6]In fact, the U. S. magazine *Health* says it is one of the five healthiest foods because it has a lot of vitamins and because it helps digestion. [7]It may even prevent cancer.[2] [8]The other four healthy foods are yogurt, olive oil, lentils, and soy. [9]Kimchi is very spicy and has a very strong taste. [10]Most Westerners have to get used to the taste, but Koreans adore it. [11]They eat it with every meal, either alone or mixed with rice or noodles. [12]They also use it in soup, pancakes, and even as a pizza topping.

Writing Assignment

Choose a word, custom, or holiday from your culture that is probably unfamiliar to an outsider. Write a paragraph to describe it and explain its meaning and/or significance. If you wish, you may use one of the topics from the Try It Out! on page 128.

Step 1 Prewrite to get ideas.

Step 2 Organize the ideas by making an outline.

Step 3 Write the rough draft. Write ROUGH DRAFT at the top of your paper.

- Focus on using good paragraph structure, with a topic sentence, supporting sentences that develop (explain) the topic, and a concluding sentence.
- Try to use at least one appositive and one adjective clause in your paragraph.

---

[1]**fermented:** allowed to rest for a period of time until chemical changes happen, such as when the sugar in grapes changes into alcohol
[2]Raymond, Joan. "World's Healthiest Foods: Kimchi (Korea). *Health* March 2006. 21 May 2006. http://www.health.com/health/article/0,23414,1149143,00.html

Step 4 Polish the rough draft.

- Exchange papers with a classmate and ask him or her to check your rough draft using Peer-Editing Worksheet 8 on page 212. Then discuss the completed worksheet and decide what changes you should make. Write a second draft.
- Use Self-Editing Worksheet 8 on page 213 to check your second draft for grammar, punctuation, and sentence structure.

Step 5 Write a final copy. Hand in your rough draft, your second draft, your final copy, and the page containing the two editing worksheets. Your teacher may also ask you to hand in your prewriting paper.

The Essay

CHAPTER 9

Essay Organization

Organization

By now, you know how to write a well-organized and well-developed paragraph. Writing an **essay** is no harder than writing a paragraph. An essay is just longer, so you have to plan it more carefully.

Three Parts of an Essay

Study the diagram and notice how the three parts of a paragraph correspond to the three parts of an essay.

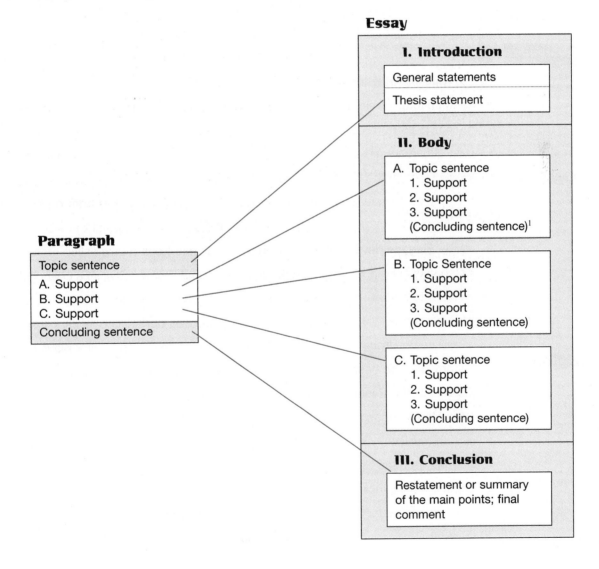

---

[1]Concluding sentences for body paragraphs in an essay are not always necessary, especially when the ideas in consecutive paragraphs are closely related.

An essay **introduction** stimulates the reader's interest and tells what the essay is about. The last sentence of an introduction is the **thesis statement**. Like the topic sentence of a paragraph, a thesis statement names the specific topic of the essay. The **body** consists of one or more paragraphs. Each paragraph develops a subdivision of the topic. The **conclusion**, like the concluding sentence in a paragraph, is a summary or review of the main points discussed in the body.

An essay has unity and coherence, just as a paragraph does. Transition signals link the paragraphs into a cohesive whole.

As you read the model essay, study its organization. Notice the transition signals at the beginning of the three body paragraphs; they tell you which pattern of organization this essay uses.

MODEL
 	
Essay Structure
 	
INTRODUCTION
 	
THESIS STATEMENT
 	
BODY PARAGRAPH 1
 	
BODY PARAGRAPH 2
	Styles of Popular Music
	
	    Music is truly the one universal language. Although all cultures have music, each culture develops its own musical forms and styles. In particular, popular music varies from culture to culture and from generation to generation. In the past 100 years or so, there has been an explosion of popular music styles in the West. Three of the more successful styles are reggae, punk, and rap.
	
	    One successful style of popular music is reggae, which was born on the Caribbean island of Jamaica in the 1960s and spread throughout the world in the 1970s. Reggae developed from a kind of Afro-Caribbean music called *mento*, which was sung and played on guitars and drums. Some musicians changed mento into a music style called *ska* by adding a hesitation beat.[1] A few years later, other musicians changed ska, and reggae was born. Reggae's special sound comes from reversing the roles of the instruments: The guitar plays the rhythm, and the bass[2] plays the melody.[3] An important influence on reggae music was the Rastafarian cult.[4] The Rastafarians added unusual sound mixes, extra-slow tempos, strange lyrics, and mystical-political themes. The best-known reggae musician was the late[5] Bob Marley. Well-known groups are Toots & The Maytals, Burning Spear, and Steel Pulse. Reggae has influenced later styles of popular music, including punk and rap.
	
	    A second successful style of popular music is punk. Punk is a style of rock music that began in the mid-1970s as a reaction against previous forms of rock.

[1]**hesitation beat:** rhythm in which one beat comes later than expected
[2]**bass:** type of guitar that plays the lowest notes of all guitars
[3]**melody:** pattern of sound that makes up a song
[4]**cult:** religious group
[5]**the late** (+ person's name): no longer living; dead

Punks felt that rock music no longer represented the counterculture[6] from which it had sprung and had, in fact, sold out[7] to the mainstream culture. With their clothing and hairstyles, punks intended to shock society. The "punk look" included spike hairdos, theatrical makeup, ripped clothing, body piercings, and jewelry made from objects such as razor blades and safety pins. The onstage behavior of punks was aggressive and provocative.[8] At concerts, fighting and other violent behavior by the fans were common occurrences. Punk music itself is simple (often just three chords), and its songs are short (rarely more than three minutes long). Its songs are anti-government, anti-authority, and anti-conformity. The first bands to popularize punk were the Sex Pistols and Clash in Great Britain and the Ramones in the United States. As with all music styles, punk has evolved[9] into other styles. Groups such as the Dead Kennedys and Black Flag play hardcore punk, which is a faster and louder punk style. The band Fall Out Boy plays emo, a style in which the musicians become so emotional during a performance that they scream and cry. Pop punk, made popular by the group Green Day, is another new punk style.

BODY PARAGRAPH 3   A third successful style of popular music is rap, which is also called *hip-hop*. Rap is a type of dance music in which the singers — rappers — speak in rhythm and rhyme rather than sing. The art of rapping originated in Africa and probably traveled to the United States via Jamaica, where it was known as *toasting*. In the United States, rap first appeared in the mid-1970s in the discos of New York City's black neighborhoods. Disco DJs[10] teamed up with rappers to play songs for dancers at parties. At first, the role of the rapper was to keep the beat[11] going with hand claps while the DJ changed records. Soon, rappers added lyrics,[12] slogans,[13] rhymes, and call-and-response exchanges with the audience, and rap was born. Early rap songs were mainly about dancing, partying, and the romantic adventures of the rappers, but politics became an important theme in rap in the late 1980s and 1990s. Most rappers are young black males, but there have been female rappers such as Queen Latifah and white rappers such as the Beastie Boys and Eminem.

---

[6]**counterculture:** culture, especially of young people, against the beliefs and values of the main culture
[7]**sold out:** went against one's beliefs and principles to gain power or money
[8]**provocative:** intended to make people angry or to cause a lot of discussion
[9]**evolved:** changed
[10]**DJs (disc jockeys):** people who play records, tapes, or CDs for dancers
[11]**beat:** rhythm
[12]**lyrics:** word to songs
[13]**slogans:** words or phrases used repeatedly, such as in advertising

CONCLUSION

> To sum up, popular music changes constantly. New styles are born, grow, change, and produce offshoots,[1] which in turn grow, change, and produce offshoots. Some styles enjoy lasting popularity, but others disappear rather quickly. However, all contribute to the power and excitement of popular music in our time.

Questions on the Model

1. How many different successful styles of popular music are discussed in the model essay? What are they?
2. How many body paragraphs are there? What is the topic of each one? Underline the topic sentences.
3. Circle the transition words and phrases that introduce the body paragraphs.
4. What pattern of organization does the essay use: logical division of ideas, process (time) order, or comparison/contrast?
5. What information is given in the supporting sentences about each style of popular music? Name at least five kinds of information (Example: how it started).

Let's examine each part of the essay.

The Introductory Paragraph

The **introductory paragraph**, or introduction, is the first paragraph of an essay. It has two functions: (1) It attracts the reader's interest, and (2) it introduces the topic of the essay.

There are several kinds of introductory paragraphs. In this book, you will learn to write a kind known as a "funnel" introduction.

A **funnel introduction** has two parts: several general statements and one thesis statement. The **general statements** give the reader background information about the topic of the essay. They should lead your reader gradually from a very general idea of your topic to a very specific idea. The first general statement in a funnel introduction just introduces the topic. Like the lens of a camera moving in for a close-up picture, each sentence that follows becomes more and more focused on a specific topic. The **thesis statement** is normally the last sentence in an introductory paragraph. It has three purposes:

1. It states the specific topic of the essay.
2. It may list the subtopics of the main topic.
3. It may also mention the method of organization.

Reread the introductory paragraph of the model essay "Styles of Popular Music." Notice how the sentences gradually move from the general topic of music to the specific topic, three successful styles of popular music.

- The first sentence attracts the reader's interest with a short sentence; it also names the general topic (music).
- The second sentence says that each culture has its own kinds of music.

---

[1]**offshoots:** branches

- The next two sentences narrow the general topic (music) to a more specific one (popular music) and mention that it has many styles.
- The final sentence, the thesis statement, specifically names the three styles to be discussed in the body paragraphs: reggae, punk, and rap.

This kind of introductory paragraph is called a *funnel introduction* because it resembles a funnel: wide at the top (beginning) and narrow at the bottom (end).

Music is truly the one universal language. Although all cultures have music, each culture develops its own musical forms and styles. In particular, popular music varies from culture to culture and from generation to generation. In the past 100 years or so, there has been an explosion of popular music styles in the West. Three of the more successful styles are reggae, punk, and rap.

PRACTICE 1

The Introductory Paragraph

In the following introductory paragraphs, the sentences are in scrambled order. On a separate piece of paper, rewrite them in the correct order. Begin with the most general statement. Then add each sentence in correct order, from the next most general to the least general. Write the thesis statement last.

1. (1) Therefore, workaholics' lifestyles can affect their families, social lives, and health. (2) Because they work so many hours, workaholics may not spend enough time in leisure activities. (3) Nowadays, many men and women work in law, accounting, real estate, and business. (4) These people are serious about becoming successful, so they work long hours during the week and even on weekends. (5) People who work long hours are called "workaholics."

2. (1) Therefore, anyone who wants to drive must carry a driver's license. (2) It is divided into four steps: studying the traffic laws, taking the written test, learning to drive, and taking the driving test. (3) Getting a driver's license is a complicated process. (4) Driving a car is a necessity in today's busy society, and it is also a special privilege.

3. (1) During this period, children separate themselves from their parents and become independent. (2) Teenagers express their separateness most vividly in their choice of clothes, hairstyles, music, and vocabulary. (3) The teenage years between childhood and adulthood are a period of growth and separation.

**Body
Paragraphs**

The body of an essay is made up of one or more paragraphs. Each **body paragraph** has a topic sentence and several supporting sentences. It may or may not have a concluding sentence. Each body paragraph supports the thesis statement.

Reread the three body paragraphs of the model essay. The topic sentence of each body paragraph introduces one style of popular music. The supporting sentences following each topic sentence give more information about each style.

Thesis statement:

Three of the more successful styles are reggae, punk, and rap.

Topic sentences:

A. One successful style of popular music is reggae, which was born on the Caribbean island of Jamaica in the 1960s and spread throughout the world in the 1970s.
B. A second successful style of popular music is punk.
C. A third successful style of popular music is rap, which is also called hip-hop.

PRACTICE 2

*Topic Sentences
for Body
Paragraphs*

For each thesis statement, write topic sentences for three supporting body paragraphs. Follow the preceding example. Use an appropriate transition signal in each topic sentence. (*Note*: You may want to use one of these topics for your own essay at the end of the chapter.)

1. Young people who live/don't live at home have several advantages.

   A. _____

   B. _____

   C. _____

2. My city/country has several interesting places to visit.

   A. _____

   B. _____

   C. _____

3. Three modern technological devices have changed the way we communicate.

   A. _____

   B. _____

   C. _____

4. There are several types of movies that I especially enjoy watching/books that I enjoy reading/sports that I enjoy playing.

   A. _____

   B. _____

   C. _____

The Concluding Paragraph

The concluding paragraph is the last paragraph of an essay. It has three purposes:

1. It signals the end of the essay.
2. It reminds the reader of your main points.
3. It leaves the reader with your final thoughts on the topic.

Notice how the writer accomplishes these three purposes in the following concluding paragraph.

> In short, Mr. Smith had several qualities of a great teacher. He was well informed about his subject, and his enthusiasm for it rubbed off on[1] his students. Furthermore, his lectures were well organized, and he returned papers and tests promptly. His classes were always interesting, and he told funny stories to keep even the sleepiest student awake and engaged in learning. Mr. Smith taught more than just history; he also taught us to love learning.

- The transition phrase *In short* signals the end of the essay.
- It summarizes the qualities of Mr. Smith: he was well informed, enthusiastic, organized, and interesting.
- It gives a final comment: Mr. Smith inspired students to love learning.

The first part of the concluding paragraph summarizes the main points or repeats the thesis statement in different words. It may require one or more than one sentence.

In the second part, you may add a final comment. This is the place to express your opinion, make a judgment, or give a recommendation. However, *do not* add any new ideas in the concluding paragraph. Just comment on what you have already discussed.

PRACTICE 3
Concluding Paragraphs

Study the following abbreviated essay outlines. Only the introductory paragraph and topic sentences for body paragraphs are given. Then circle the number of the most appropriate concluding paragraph.

1. **Advertising**

Unless you live on an uninhabited island in the middle of a big ocean, you cannot escape advertising. People in the modern world are continually exposed to ads and commercials on the radio, on television, on billboards, in their mailboxes, and on their computers. However, advertising is not a modern phenomenon. Advertising has been around for a long time, as a review of its history shows.

(continued on next page)

---

[1] **rubbed off on:** transferred itself to (informal)

A. As early as 3000 B.C., merchants carved signs in wood, clay, and stone to put above their shops.

B. In ancient Egypt, merchants hired people called criers to walk through the streets announcing the arrival of ships and their cargo.

C. In medieval Europe, shop owners hired criers to direct customers to their shops.

D. The invention of the printing press was the start of the advertising industry as we know it today.

Possible concluding paragraphs

(1) As we have seen, advertising has been a part of merchandising for at least 5,000 years. From the carved signs above doorways in ancient Babylonia to the annoying pop-ups on modern computer screens, advertising has been a part of daily life. Its form may change, but advertising will undoubtedly be with us for a long time to come.

(2) It is clear that advertising is useful for both buyers and sellers. It helps sellers by informing the public about their goods and services. It helps buyers by allowing them to comparison shop. Its form may change, but advertising will undoubtedly be with us for a long time to come.

2.   **Compulsory[1] Attendance in College**

On my first day of class in an American university, I discovered that there are many differences between universities in the United States and in my country. One difference hit me immediately when the professor walked into the classroom dressed in casual pants and a sports shirt. Then he sat down, and I received a second shock. He sat down *on* the desk, not behind the desk. The biggest shock happened when he passed out a piece of paper listing the requirements of the class. I learned that I was not allowed to miss any classes! In my country, professors do not know or care if students attend lectures, but in the United States, professors actually call the roll[2] at the beginning of each class meeting. In my opinion, compulsory attendance in college is completely inappropriate for two reasons.

A. College students are adults, not elementary school children.

B. Students often have other obligations such as jobs and family.

---

[1]**compulsory:** required
[2]**call the roll:** say the names of students to find out who is present or absent

Possible concluding paragraphs

(1) To summarize, attendance in college classes should be optional. Students may already know the material that the professor will cover. Sometimes the professor lectures on material that is in the textbook, so students can read it on their own time. Therefore, in my opinion, compulsory attendance in college classes should be abolished.

(2) To summarize, college students are mature enough to take charge of their own learning. Furthermore, they may have family or work problems once in a while that cause them to miss a class. They should not be penalized for this. Therefore, in my opinion, compulsory attendance in college classes should be abolished.

3.
Goals

Everyone needs goals. Having goals makes you more successful because they keep your mind on what is really important to you. However, goals can change at different times in your life. Your goals when you are ten are very different from your goals at fifteen or twenty. My major goals this semester are to get a part-time job and to master the use of the English language.

   A. My first goal is to get a part-time job in an area related to my field of study.

   B. I also plan to improve my ability to speak, write, read, and understand English.

Possible concluding paragraphs

(1) In conclusion, it is important to have goals. When you have clear goals, it is easier to stay focused and not let small things sidetrack you. I hope I succeed in reaching my goals this semester.

(2) In conclusion, finding a job and using English well are important to me at this stage of my life. I am working hard to succeed at both.

(3) In conclusion, I have set important goals for myself this semester. If I do not reach my goals, I will be unhappy. Next semester, I will have new goals.

4.
Changes in the Workplace

Female airline pilots? Male nurses? When my parents were young, such job descriptions were not possible. In the past thirty-five years, however, society has become more accepting. Although it is still somewhat unusual, men now work in traditionally female occupations. In particular, more and more men are becoming nurses, secretaries, and elementary school teachers.

A. The nursing profession has seen the greatest increase in male participation.

B. Besides nursing, more men are becoming secretaries.

C. Elementary school teaching is a third occupation that men are taking up.

Possible concluding paragraphs

(1) These examples have shown that it is no longer unusual to see men working as nurses, secretaries, and elementary school teachers. As society continues to change, we will undoubtedly see this trend continue.

(2) These examples have shown that it is no longer unusual to see men working as nurses, secretaries, and elementary school teachers. On the other hand, it is no longer unusual to find women engineers, construction supervisors, and corporate CEOs.[1] In fact, there are already more women than men studying to become lawyers.

(3) These examples have shown that it is no longer unusual to see men working as nurses, secretaries, and elementary school teachers. Indeed, there is less sexism in the working world as men have proven themselves to be as capable as women in these areas, and women have proven themselves to be as capable as men in others.

Transitions Between Paragraphs

Just as it is important to use transition signals to show the connection between ideas *within* a paragraph, it is also important to use transition signals *between* paragraphs to show how one paragraph is related to another. Transition signals can tell your reader if the topic of the next paragraph follows the same line of thought or reverses direction.

In addition to costing money for special food, fad diets . . .

On the other hand, fad diets work for some people . . .

The writer of these sentences could have used any of the transition signals in the chart that follows. The four on the left are ones that you already know. The two on the right are new. The advantage of using the new ones is that you can repeat the topic of the preceding paragraph in the same sentence in which you name the topic of the next paragraph. This technique helps link your body paragraphs into a coherent, cohesive essay.

Notice that *Besides* appears in both lists. In the list on the left, *Besides* is a sentence connector and must be followed by a comma and an independent clause. In the list on the right, *Besides* is a preposition and must be followed by a noun or gerund.[2] Similarly, *In addition* is a sentence connector, and *In addition to* is a preposition.

---

[1] **CEOs:** chief executive officers, the title of the top person in a corporation
[2] **gerund:** -*ing* word used as a noun, such as *swimming* or *shopping*

"Additional Idea" Transition Signals

Sentence Connectors	Prepositions
1. Furthermore, . . . Moreover, . . . Besides, . . . In addition, . . .	2. Besides (+ noun or gerund) . . . In addition to (+ noun or gerund) . . .

1. **Furthermore / In addition / Moreover / Besides,** people on fad diets often gain even more weight than they had lost.

   Besides / In addition to suffering from poor nutrition, people on fad diets often don't lose weight. (The word *suffering* is a gerund.)

2. **Besides / In addition to not losing weight,** people on fad diets often gain even more weight than they had lost.

If the next paragraph is about an opposite idea, use one of the following transitions.

"Opposite Idea" Transition Signals

Sentence Connectors	Subordinators	Prepositions
1. On the other hand, . . . However, . . .	2. Although . . . Even though . . .	3. Despite . . . In spite of . . .

1. **On the other hand / However,** people who want to lose weight can succeed.

2. **Although / Even though** fad diets do not work, there are other diets that do.

3. **Despite / In spite of** many attempts to lose weight, I am still overweight.

   Despite / In spite of dieting for several years, I am still overweight.

PRACTICE 4

Transitions Between Paragraphs

Add appropriate transition signals to the beginning of each paragraph (except the introductory paragraph) in the following essay.

Step 1 Read the entire essay.

Step 2 Decide the relationship of each body paragraph to the preceding one. Is it an additional idea or an opposite idea?

Step 3 Choose appropriate transition signals for paragraphs 3–8 and write them on the lines. Use a different transition in each one. Punctuate carefully. You may have to rewrite the entire sentence.

The Computer Revolution

1   We live in the age of technology. Every day, new technology appears, ranging from iPods that can store thousands of songs to giant space telescopes that can send photographs of distant stars back to Earth. Of all the new

technological wonders, personal computers have probably had the greatest influence on the daily lives of average people. Through computers, we can now talk to people in any country, research any topic, work, shop, bank, and entertain ourselves. Personal computers have especially revolutionized communication, business practices, and education in both positive and negative ways.

2   Perhaps the most important effect of personal computers has been to expand our ability to communicate with the outside world. A lonely invalid[1] in Minnesota can talk with a similarly house-bound[2] person in Mississippi. A single computer user can send an e-mail message to millions of people all over the world with one keystroke. Computer users can get together in an online chat room to discuss their interests and problems with others who have similar interests and problems. For example, a person who is planning a vacation and wants to know the names of the best beaches in Costa Rica can ask others who have already been there for suggestions. People even start romances through online dating services! The possibilities of computerized communication are indeed unlimited.

3   _____, personal computers are changing the way we do business. One change is that computers make it easy to take care of a lot of personal business at home. For example, you can buy airline tickets, send a greeting card, pay bills, buy and sell almost anything, and even pay your taxes from your home computer at any time of the day or night. This is a great convenience for people who are busy during the day and for physically disabled people who find it hard to leave their homes.

4   _____ telecommuting — working at home instead of going to the office — has become a choice for thousands of businesspeople. Suzanne Carreiro, a financial manager for a large company in downtown Manhattan, has telecommuted from her home in New Jersey for the past two years. She goes to her office only once a week. Four days a week, she works at home and communicates with her staff by computer.

5   _____ personal computers have changed the world of education. Elementary schoolchildren are learning to write, practice math, and create art on the computer. Schoolchildren in Manhattan can talk via computer to schoolchildren in Moscow. High school and college students no longer need

---

[1]**invalid:** sick person
[2]**house-bound:** having to stay inside the house

to spend hours in the school library researching topics for term papers. A high school student can obtain statistics for a history paper from a library in London by computer.

6 _____, not everyone agrees that computers are good for education. Replacing a teacher with a machine is not progress, according to some critics. They say that young children especially need a real person, not a machine, to guide their learning.

7 _____ computers have caused problems for society. People who spend hours each day surfing the Internet can become isolated and lonely, and children and teenagers can meet strangers through the Internet who may be dangerous.

8 _____ the computer age has arrived, and it has changed our lives. Computers have made communicating and doing business faster and more convenient, and they are changing the way we learn in school. Just as the invention of automobiles had an unplanned consequence — the growth of suburbs — so will the invention of personal computers. We will have to wait and see what unintended consequences may develop.

Essay Outlining

Making an outline is even more important when you are planning an essay because you have many more ideas and details to organize. An outline for an essay with two body paragraphs might look like this.

MODEL

Essay Outline

I. Introduction
   Thesis statement

II. Body

   A. Topic Sentence
      1. Main Supporting Point
         a. Supporting Detail
         b. Supporting Detail
      2. Main Supporting Point
         a. Supporting Detail
         b. Supporting Detail
      3. Main Supporting Point
         a. Supporting Detail
         b. Supporting Detail

> B. Topic Sentence
>   1. Main Supporting Point
>   a. Supporting Detail
>   b. Supporting Detail
>   2. Main Supporting Point
>   a. Supporting Detail
>   b. Supporting Detail
>
> III. Conclusion

Notice these points:

1. The introduction, body, and conclusion are numbered with Roman numerals: I, II, and III.
2. The topic sentence of each body paragraph is given a capital letter (A, B, C, and so on).
3. Each main supporting point is numbered 1, 2, 3, and so on.
4. Each supporting detail is given a small letter (a, b, c, and so on).
5. Each time the outline moves from a Roman numeral to a capital letter to an Arabic numeral, the text is indented. Indenting makes it easy to see the movement from big to small, from main points to specific details.

PRACTICE 5

Outlining an Essay

Complete the following outline for the model essay on pages 148–150. Notice that the thesis statement, first topic sentence, and concluding sentences are written out in full. You should write out topic sentences in full, but you may use short phrases to list supporting points and supporting details if you wish.

Outline: Styles of Popular Music

I. Introduction

Thesis Statement: Three of the more successful styles are reggae, punk, and rap.

II. Body

A. One successful style of popular music is reggae.

  1. Born on the Caribbean island of Jamaica in the 1960s.

     a. _____

  2. Developed from *mento*.

     a. _____

     b. _____

  3. _____

     a. Guitar plays rhythm and bass plays melody.

4. _____

    a. Unusual sound mixes

    b. _____

    c. _____

    d. _____

5. Bob Marley—best known reggae musician

    a. _____

6. _____

B. _____

1. _____

    a. _____

2. With clothing and hairstyles, punks intended to shock society.

    a. _____

3. _____

    a. _____

4. Punk music is simple.

    a. _____

    b. _____

    c. _____

5. _____

6. Punk has evolved into other styles.

    a. _____

    b. _____

    c. _____

C. A third successful style of popular music is rap.

1. Also known as hip-hop

2. Form of dance music—singers speak in rhythm and rhyme

3. Originated in Africa

    a. Traveled to the U.S. via Jamaica—"toasting"

    b. _____

    c. Disco DJs + rappers played songs for dancers at parties

    d. _____

    e. _____

4. _____

    a. Politics—theme in 1980s and 1990s

5. _____

    a. Female rapper—Queen Latifah

    b. _____

III. Conclusion

Popular music changes constantly. New styles are born, grow, change, and produce offshoots, which in turn grow, change, and produce offshoots. Some styles enjoy lasting popularity, but others disappear rather quickly. However, all contribute to the power and excitement of popular music in our time.

Planning an Essay

Planning an essay takes a little more work because there are many ideas and details to organize. Let's review the steps in the writing process that were introduced in Chapter 1.

Step 1
Prewriting

In this step, you choose a topic and then gather supporting ideas and details. There are several ways to gather ideas, including listing, clustering, freewriting, journal writing, interviewing classmates and friends, researching online, and researching in a library.

Here is an example of the listing technique. The topic is "Kinds of Lies." Notice that the list is not in any order. The writer just wrote down any idea or example that came to mind.

Kinds of Lies

good lies	broken window
bad lies	stole a cookie
different motives (reasons)	stole a bicycle
social lies	lying to police officer when caught speeding
lies to get out of trouble	
lies to save face	lying on a job application
lies to avoid punishment	lying to avoid hurting someone's feelings
polite lies	
diplomatic lies	bad haircut
helpful lies	clothes that don't fit, don't look good, or are out of style
friend who failed an important exam	
friend who didn't get the job he/she wanted	lies that hurt someone's feelings
children who do something bad	malicious lies that harm another person

Step 2
Organizing

In the second step of the writing process, you organize your ideas. First, you divide your ideas into categories or groups. You may delete some ideas and add others. Then you make an outline and add specific details as necessary.

Step 2A Group Ideas Logically

The first step in organizing is to group your ideas logically.

PRACTICE 6

Grouping Ideas Logically

Work with a classmate, a small group, or the entire class.

A. Divide the following list of words into the logical groups or categories on the chart. Write each word under the appropriate category name.

Shopping in a Supermarket

aspirin	cheese	cookies	tomatoes
bread	lettuce	eggs	steak
apples	potatoes	hamburger	cake
carrots	vitamins	pork chops	toothpaste
oranges	pie	shampoo	doughnuts
milk			

Produce	Dairy Products	Meat	Baked Goods	Personal Care/ Health Products

B. Divide the list of sports into groups. There is more than one possible way to divide the list. First, decide with your partner or group what your categories will be and label the chart columns. You may have more or fewer categories than there are columns in the chart. If you need more columns or more space in each column, add them.

Sports

badminton	fishing	jogging	swimming
baseball	golf	mountain climbing	table tennis
basketball	gymnastics	scuba diving	tennis
bobsledding	hiking	skateboarding	volleyball
bowling	ice hockey	skiing	waterskiing
diving	ice skating	soccer	windsurfing

C. On a separate piece of paper, divide the list of "Kinds of Lies" into logical groups or categories. Some items may not fit in any category; delete them. Also, some items may be examples; either delete them or put them in a category.

Step 2B Make an Outline

The second step in organizing is to make an outline.

PRACTICE 7

Outlining Body Paragraphs

Work together with a classmate, a small group, or the entire class.

A. Make an outline *of the body paragraphs only* for an essay about different kinds of sports. Use the categories you selected as topics for separate paragraphs.

B. Make an outline *of the body paragraphs only* for an essay about different kinds of lies. Use the categories you developed as topics for separate paragraphs. Add examples as necessary.

Review

These are the important points covered in this chapter:

1. The organization of an essay is similar to the organization of a paragraph; it is just longer.

2. An essay has three parts: an introduction, a body, and a conclusion.

   • The introduction (or introductory paragraph) introduces the topic of the essay and arouses the reader's interest. It always contains one sentence that clearly states the main idea of the whole essay. This sentence is called the *thesis statement*.

- The body of an essay is made up of one or more paragraphs. Each body paragraph explains or develops one part of the essay topic.
- The conclusion is the last paragraph. It summarizes the main points of the essay.

3. It is important to use transitions to show how one body paragraph is related to the preceding one.

4. Because an essay is longer than a paragraph, it requires more careful planning. Always make an outline.

Skill Sharpeners

The following exercise will help you review important skills you learned in prior chapters:

EXERCISE
Sentence Structure Review

Edit the following essay for errors in sentence structure. Find and correct two comma splices, one run-on, and five fragments. (Review fragments on pages 14–15 in Chapter 1; review comma splices and run-ons on pages 87–90 in Chapter 5.)

Left-Handedness

Do you know anyone who is left-handed? You probably do, about 10 percent of the population uses their left rather than their right hand for writing and other tasks. Although many athletes, musicians, artists, and world leaders are left-handed, being left-handed certainly has a few disadvantages in a world designed by and for right-handed people.

Social situations can provide opportunities for left-handed people to feel clumsy. First of all, handshakes. Right-handed people offer their right hands and expect to grasp the right hand of the other person. The instinct of left-handers, however, is to extend their left hand they have to train themselves to extend their right. Another social opportunity for awkwardness occurs at the dinner table. Left-handed diners constantly bump elbows with a right-handed person. Unless they sit at the far end of the table with no one on their left. What's worse, left-handers have to concentrate in order to avoid grabbing and drinking from the wrong glass.

Left-handed people can face inconveniences at school, too. Consider the chairs in classrooms with little fold-up desktops for taking notes. Most of them are made for right-handers. Left-handers have to write with their left elbow hanging in midair. Or else turn themselves around almost 180 degrees in order to lay their notebook on the desk. Furthermore, when lefties write in a three-ring binder or spiral notebook. The rings get in the way of their hands when they write on the front side of a page. Finally, left-handers write from left to right, their hand smears the fresh ink across the page.

Last but not least are the many inventions of the modern world. That make life convenient for right-handers but inconvenient for lefties. These include scissors, can openers, corkscrews, automobile gear shifts, cameras, and computer keyboards.

In sum, in a world organized for right-handers, left-handed people must confront and overcome challenges every day.

Writing Assignment

Choose one of the topics from Practice 2 on page 152 *or* one of the alternative topics suggested.

Step 1 Prewrite to get ideas.

Step 2 Organize the ideas by making an outline.

Step 3 Write the rough draft. Write ROUGH DRAFT at the top of your paper.

Step 4 Polish the rough draft.

- Exchange papers with a classmate and ask him or her to check your rough draft using Peer-Editing Worksheet 9 on page 214. Then discuss the completed worksheet and decide what changes you should make. Write a second draft.
- Use Self-Editing Worksheet 9 on page 215 to check your second draft for grammar, punctuation, and sentence structure.

Step 5 Write a final copy. Hand in your rough draft, your second draft, your final copy, and the page containing the two editing worksheets. Your teacher may also ask you to hand in your prewriting paper.

Alternative Writing Topics

kinds of customers/shoppers/automobile drivers/teachers/students/sports fans
daredevil sports/new sports
styles of popular music/Latino music/jazz music/dance music

clothing styles/hair styles/ shoe styles
television programs worth watching/not worth watching
jobs I would be good at

Summary Writing II

Writing a summary of a longer piece of writing, such as an essay or magazine article, is an important skill. College teachers often assign research papers (also called *term papers* because students usually have an entire term to complete them). To write a research paper, you will have to read articles from outside sources and use information that you get from these readings in your paper. One way to use this information is to use quotations. Another way is to summarize information.

When you summarize a longer piece of writing, you use the same techniques you used for summarizing a short paragraph.

1. Write the important ideas, and leave out most of the details.
2. Do not summarize the concluding paragraph because it is already a summary of the main points or a restatement of the main idea.
3. Use as few words as possible without omitting important points.
4. Use your own words. Do not copy sentences from the original.

Here is an example of a summary of "The Computer Revolution" on pages 157–159.

Summary of "The Computer Revolution"

Computers have changed the way we communicate, do business, and educate our children in both good and bad ways. We now communicate through e-mail, chat rooms, and online dating services. We can also shop online and work at home. Computers in schools allow students to practice new skills, exchange ideas with students in other parts of the world, and do research more easily. Computers have negative effects, too. Some people spend too much time surfing the Net, and there is the danger of meeting bad people online. Also, some people say that computers should not replace teachers in elementary schools.

PRACTICE 8

Summarizing an Essay

Write a summary of any of the essays in this chapter. Begin by rewriting the thesis statement in your own words. Then summarize each body paragraph in one or two sentences. Your completed summary should be one paragraph in length.

"Styles of Popular Music," pages 148–150
"Left-Handedness," pages 165–166

Opinion Essays

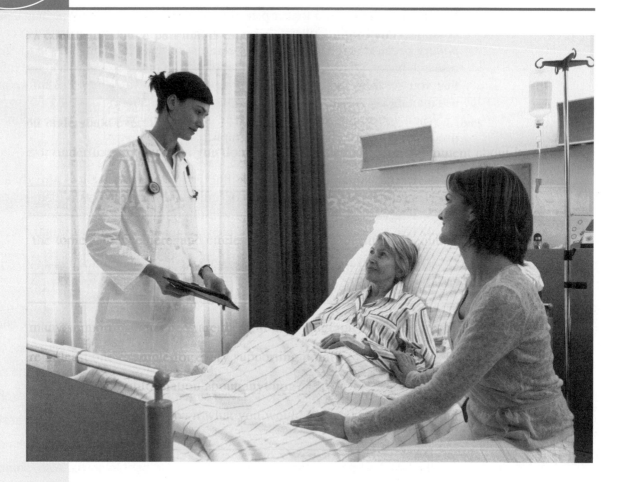

Organization

In our daily lives, we express opinions about everything from politics to the cost of gasoline. When we express an opinion, we usually give reasons for our point of view in an informal way. For example, we say, "I liked XYZ's latest movie because . . ." or "I voted against XYZ because . . . ."

In college classes, students are often asked to express their opinions more formally. The U.S. system of education places a high value on students' ability to think for themselves. Professors want students to express their own opinions and even disagree with them as long as students can support their own views. In this chapter, you will learn how to express an opinion and support it convincingly.

In an **opinion essay**, you

- state your opinion in the thesis statement.
- support your opinion with reasons.
- support your reasons with specific details.

As you read the model essay, notice its three parts: introduction, body, and conclusion.

MODEL	**The Right to Die**
Opinion Essay	
INTRODUCTION	A difficult problem that is facing society is the legalization of euthanasia. Euthanasia is the act of causing death painlessly in order to end suffering. People who are in a coma[1] because of injury to their brains and elderly people who are terminally[2] ill are being kept alive by artificial means. They do not have a chance to recover, but laws in most states of the United States do not allow doctors to end their lives. Although many people feel that doctors must do everything possible to
THESIS STATEMENT	keep their patients alive, I believe that euthanasia should be legal for three reasons.
BODY PARAGRAPH 1	The first and most important reason to support euthanasia is that some patients who have no chance to recover do not wish to be kept alive on machines. These patients are kept alive by life-support machines such as respirators to help them breathe and feeding tubes to provide them with nutrition. A well-known example in the United States is the case of Terri Schiavo, a young woman who went into a coma in 1990. Mrs. Schiavo was able to breathe on her own, but her brain was dead. For fifteen years, she was kept alive by a feeding tube. After eight years of seeking treatment for her condition, Michael Schiavo, her husband, asked the courts for permission to remove her feeding tube. He said that his wife had

---

[1]**coma:** unconscious state (cannot see, hear, or speak)
[2]**terminally ill:** having no chance of getting well

told him she would not want to be kept alive artificially when there was no hope of recovery. Mrs. Schiavo's parents, Robert and Mary Schindler, disagreed with Mr. Schiavo and fought to keep their daughter alive. After seven years of bitter court battles, Mr. Schiavo finally won. Doctors removed Mrs. Schiavo's feeding tube, and she soon died, fifteen years after first falling into a coma. Clearly, when there is absolutely no hope of recovery, society should allow a person in Terri Schiavo's condition to die if that is his or her wish.

BODY PARAGRAPH 2

A second reason to support euthanasia is that medical costs in the United States are very high. Keeping a person alive for years and years requires round-the-clock care in a hospital or nursing home.[1] According to an administrator at a local hospital, daily hospital room charges average $5,000 there. Nursing home care is also expensive. A nursing home in our area charges $4,500 per month. These high costs can cause serious financial problems for a family.

BODY PARAGRAPH 3

The final reason to support legalizing euthanasia is that the family suffers. Hospital or nursing home staff give terminally ill patients only minimal care. Thus, the family must spend time caring for the special needs of their loved one. For instance, a cousin of mine who had been in a motorcycle accident was kept on life-support machines for eight years. He needed someone to stay with him twenty-four hours a day. During those years, his parents took turns taking care of him. His father stayed with him during the day while his mother worked, and then his mother stayed with him at night while his father worked. Other family members tried to help out when they could, but his parents did most of the physical work and suffered most of the emotional stress. After he finally died, my aunt said, "Of course, I am sad, but since we all knew he would eventually die, it might have been better if it had happened right when he had the accident. These past eight years have been hard."

CONCLUSION

To summarize, patients who are either terminally ill or who are in an irreversible[2] coma often wish to die. Their care is a financial, physical, and emotional burden for their families. Therefore, families should have the right to ask doctors to turn off life-support machines or to remove feeding tubes.

---

[1]**nursing home:** place where people who are too old or sick to take care of themselves can live
[2]**irreversible:** cannot be reversed, cannot be changed

Questions on the Model
1. In the introduction, which sentence expresses the writer's opinion about the right to die? Double-underline it. How many body paragraphs can the reader expect?
2. How many body paragraphs are there? Underline the topic sentences, and circle the transition signals that introduce each paragraph.
3. Which body paragraph has a concluding sentence?
4. Does the concluding paragraph summarize the reasons, or does it repeat the thesis statement?

The Introductory Paragraph

Remember that an introductory paragraph has two parts: (1) several general statements and (2) one thesis statement. The first part of the introductory paragraph of an opinion essay often begins by explaining an issue.

GENERAL STATEMENTS

> In some cities in the United States, teenage gangs create problems. The problems range from noisy but harmless drag races[3] to fatal drive-by shootings.[4] Some cities are trying to stop these activities by keeping young people indoors and off the streets at night. These cities have passed curfew laws that require people under the age of eighteen to be indoors between the hours of 10:00 or 11:00 P.M. and 6:00 A.M.

The thesis statement then states the writer's opinion on the issue. It often mentions the opposing view first.

THESIS STATEMENT

> Police departments say that curfew laws to control teenage gangs are necessary, but I feel that such laws are unfair, unconstitutional, and counterproductive.[5]

Notice that the opposing view is connected to the writer's opinion with a contrast signal such as *however*, *but*, and *although*. (Review contrast signals on pages 114 and 118–120.)

PRACTICE 1

Thesis Statements for Opinion Essays

A. Turn back to the model essay "The Right to Die" on pages 169–170, and find the thesis statement. What contrast signal connects the opposing opinions?

B. What contrast signal connects the opposing opinions in the above example about curfew laws?

C. Work alone, with a classmate, or in a small group. Complete each thesis statement by adding the opposite opinion. Notice that statements 3 and 6 require a separate sentence.

Note: You may want to use one of these topics for your own essay at the end of this chapter.

---

[3]**drag races:** informal automobile races
[4]**drive-by shootings:** gun shootings from a moving vehicle
[5]**counterproductive:** leading to a result that is the opposite of the result desired or intended

1. Although the law prohibits separate classes for boys and girls in public schools, <u>I think boys and girls learn better in separate classes, especially in the middle grades.</u>

2. Many people believe that women should not serve in the military, but _____
   _____

3. Society often ignores steroid use by well-known professional athletes because of the athletes' popularity. However,_____
   _____

4. Although professional athletes undoubtedly feel that they deserve their million-dollar salaries, I feel _____
   _____

5. Some people are in favor of drug testing for high school athletes, but _____
   _____

6. Some people feel that the United States needs more laws to control the sale and ownership of guns. However,_____
   _____

Try It Out!

Choose one of the suggested topics and write an introductory paragraph for an opinion essay about it. *Note*: You may want to use one of these topics for your own essay at the end of this chapter.

Step 1 Discuss the topic with a classmate, a small group, or the entire class until you understand the problem or issue. Discuss both sides of the issue.

Step 2 Decide whether you are *for* or *against* the issue.

Step 3 Then write an explanation of the issue as the first part of your introductory paragraph.

Step 4 Write a thesis statement as the last sentence of your introductory paragraph. Be sure to mention the opposing view.

Topic Suggestions

any topic from Practice 1
school uniforms
dress codes in schools
arranged marriages
antismoking laws
laws against cell phone use while
driving
required homework/attendance in
college or university classes

grades in university classes
antiterrorism regulations
censorship of films, song lyrics,
books, video games, or television
programs
genetically engineered food
_____ (a topic of your
own choosing)

Body Paragraphs

In the body paragraphs, support your opinion with reasons. Each reason is a paragraph in the finished essay.

THESIS STATEMENT Although many people feel that doctors must do everything possible to keep their patients alive, I believe that euthanasia should be legalized for three reasons.

REASON A These patients have no chance of recovery.

REASON B Medical costs are very high.

REASON C The family suffers.

PRACTICE 2
Developing Reasons

Choose three thesis statements from Practice 1 on page 171 or the Try It Out! exercise on page 172. Write down at least three reasons to support each one.

1. Thesis statement: _____

   Reason A: _____

   Reason B: _____

   Reason C: _____

2. Thesis statement: _____

   Reason A: _____

   Reason B: _____

   Reason C: _____

3. Thesis statement: _____

   Reason A: _____

   Reason B: _____

   Reason C: _____

The Concluding Paragraph

In the concluding paragraph, you may (1) restate your thesis in different words or (2) summarize your reasons. In your final comment, you may call for action, as in the following example. Your final comment should be powerful—one that your readers will remember.

> To summarize, cloning humans is clearly dangerous and unethical. It is one thing to clone a mouse, sheep, or pig but quite another thing to duplicate a human being. Even though scientists claim that their only purpose is to help humanity, ethical people must demand an end to such experiments now.

Try It Out!

Write a concluding paragraph for one of the items from Practice 2 on page 173.

Developing Supporting Details

In Chapter 3, you learned how to use examples to support your ideas. In this chapter, you will learn how to use three other kinds of supporting details: quotations, statistics, and summaries.

College instructors often assign research papers in their classes, for which you use information from outside sources (books, magazines, newspaper articles, or the Internet). There are special procedures and rules for using information from outside sources. For example, in a formal research paper, you must document the source of each piece of information that you use. This means that you must tell exactly where you got the information—who originally wrote it or said it and when and where it was written or spoken. You will learn how to do this later on in your college program. However, be aware that documenting outside sources is important and necessary for college assignments.

For purposes of this class, you may get information informally—by taking a class survey to get statistics or by interviewing classmates to get quotations, for example.

Quotations

Quotations are often used in academic writing as supporting sentences. Notice how quotations support the topic sentence in the following paragraphs.

> Telecommuting[1] is a popular new choice for many office workers. They feel it offers advantages to both employees and employers. My older sister, who has telecommuted for the past year, told me, "I am much more productive when I work at home because there are no interruptions. I also don't have to spend two or three hours traveling to and from the office every day. I save myself time, and I save my company money by working at home."

> On the other hand, sometimes telecommuters feel isolated. "I feel out of touch with[2] what is really happening in my company, and I miss the daily contact with my co-workers," my sister added.

---

[1]**telecommuting:** working at home, usually by using a computer to produce work and to communicate
[2]**out of touch with:** not in communication with

Rules for Using and Punctuating Quotations

Rule	Example
1. Use a "reporting phrase" such as *she says*, *she said*, *he stated*, *he added*, *he continued*, or *they reported*. The reporting phrase may come before, after, or in the middle of the quotation, and the verb may be in any appropriate tense. Separate a quotation from a reporting phrase with commas. Another useful reporting phrase is *according to* followed by the name of the source. If you copy words exactly, use quotation marks.	"I like you," **he said.** **He said,** "I like you." "I like you," **he said,** "but I don't like your dog. He's a pit bull." **According to** veterinarian Dr. James Brown, "Pit bulls are unpredictable and dangerous dogs."
2. Begin each quoted sentence with a capital letter. . When a quoted sentence is separated into two parts, begin the second part with a small letter	"**Y**our dog is a pit bull," he continued, "**a**nd I am afraid of him."
3. Commas, periods, question marks, and exclamation points go inside the second quotation mark of a pair.	She said, "Good-bye." "Don't call me again," she continued. "Why not?" he asked. She answered, "I don't go out with people who don't like my dog!"
4. Give the quoted person's title or occupation if he or she is not well known. The easiest way to do this is to put the information in an appositive. (Review appositives on pages 128–131 in Chapter 8.)	My older sister, **financial manager for a large insurance company,** claims, "I save myself time, and I save my company money by telecommuting." **Classmate** Jessica Wang said, "My children don't realize that the violence they see on television is fiction. They think it is real."

PRACTICE 3

Punctuating Quotations

Punctuate the following sentences containing quotations. Add quotation marks, commas, and capital letters.

1. Dr. T. Berry Brazelton said the average child today spends more time in front of a TV set than she does studying in school or talking with her parents.

2. as a result he added children often learn more about the world and about values from television than from their families.

3. a majority of child characters on ABC, NBC, CBS, and Fox programs tend to engage in antisocial behavior such as lying or physical aggression reported Damon Ho, president of Parents for Responsible Programming.

4. advice columnist Abigail van Buren wrote in a recent column the television set may provide some people with the only human voice they hear for days.

5. it provides news and entertainment for millions of people who cannot leave the comfort, privacy, and safety of their homes she continued.

6. not everyone can attend college in a traditional way says Greenhills College professor Caroline Gibbs so we televise courses that students can view on their TV sets at home.

Statistics

Like quotations, **statistics** are an excellent kind of supporting detail. Suppose you want to prove that talking on a cell phone while driving is dangerous. You could go online or to a library and find statistics about the number of traffic accidents that happen when people use cell phones while driving.

Use statistics in the same way you use quotations. Use a reporting phrase such as *Statistics show that . . .* or *Statistical data prove that . . .* or *A survey of our class shows that . . . .*

> **Statistics prove** that people find the use of cell phones annoying. **According to** a survey of our class, 85 percent of the students had been bothered by a cell phone ringing or by a stranger talking on a cell phone in the past week. Eighteen (of forty) students had heard a cell phone ring in an inappropriate place such as a movie theater or a library study room. Five students reported that they had been forced to listen to private conversations while riding in elevators. Nine listed other violations of cell phone etiquette during the past week.

PRACTICE 4

Supporting Details

Turn back to the model essay "The Right to Die" on pages 169–170.

1. What kind of supporting details does the writer give in the first body paragraph: examples, statistics, and/or quotations?
2. What kind of supporting details does the writer give in the second body paragraph?
3. What kind of supporting details does the writer give in the third body paragraph?

Try It Out!

Practice using quotations and statistics.

A. Everyone agrees that television has had a tremendous influence on society since it was developed in the 1940s. Some influences have been positive, but others have been negative. With your entire class or in a small group, brainstorm the influences of television. Brainstorm both positive and negative influences. Think about how television has changed communication, education, and family life. Make two lists.

Positive Influences	Negative Influences
_____	_____
_____	_____
_____	_____
_____	_____
_____	_____
_____	_____
_____	_____

B. Read the following interviews about some positive and negative effects of television:

Does TV Improve the Quality of Life?

Interviews with New Yorkers

Harry Wang, grocery store manager: With proper programming, TV can be good. Educational channels are excellent. You can learn about foreign cultures, wild animals, and all sorts of things from the comfort of your living room. Children's educational shows such as *Sesame Street* are good, too. My daughter learned her ABCs from watching Big Bird and his friends.

Jessica Wang, housewife: No! Television is destroying family life. Now families just sit like robots in front of the boob tube[1] instead of talking or playing games together. Some families even eat dinner in front of the TV screen. There's little communication between parents and their children or even between husband and wife except maybe an argument about whether to watch *Monday Night Football* or *ER*.

Angela Russell, nurse: TV is a great source of entertainment and companionship for old people. My eighty-six-year-old mother is in a wheelchair and has nothing to do all day. She loves watching the soap operas in the morning and the game shows in the afternoon. Without them, she would really be bored. I think these programs keep her mind active.

Jacques Camembert, recent immigrant: Television is helping me and my family learn English more quickly. When we first came to the United States, we could not understand anything. We stayed in our apartment and watched television all day. At first, we watched children's shows, which were easier to understand. Now we can understand a lot more. We are learning the way Americans really talk, not "textbook" English.

George Russell, engineer: You bet! My kids have learned so much from watching educational programs such as the Discovery Channel and the National Geographic specials. My daughter became interested in science from watching the Science Channel, and my son wants to become a chef because of all the excellent cooking shows he watches.

---

[1]**boob tube:** television set

C. Choose two influences (positive or negative) that you and your classmates brainstormed in Part A and write a paragraph about each. Use at least one quotation from the interviews in each paragraph.

Review

These are the important points covered in this chapter:

1. In an opinion essay, you explain your opinion about a controversial topic.

- In the first part of the introduction, briefly explain the issue.
- In the thesis statement, state your opinion. You may also briefly mention the opposite opinion in your thesis statement.
- Support your opinion with reasons. Write about a different reason in each body paragraph.
- Support each reason with details such as quotations, statistics, and examples.

2. In academic papers, you often use information from outside sources. You must always tell where you found the information.

- Use reporting phrases such as *Classmate John Smith says*, . . . or *According to a class survey*, . . . to give the source of your information.
- Put quotation marks around words that you copy exactly.

Skill Sharpeners

The following exercises will help you review important skills you learned in prior chapters.

EXERCISE 1

Outlining

Complete the outline of the model essay "The Right to Die" on pages 169–170 with the supporting details. Notice that the supporting details are examples, statistics, or quotations.

THESIS STATEMENT

Although many people feel that doctors must do everything possible to keep their patients alive, I believe that euthanasia should be legal for three reasons.

A. The first and most important reason to support euthanasia is that some patients who have no chance to recover do not wish to be kept alive on machines

EXAMPLE

1. Terry Schiavo's story _____

B. Medical costs are very high.

STATISTIC 1. _____

STATISTIC 2. _____

C. The family suffers.

EXAMPLE 1. _____

QUOTATION 2. _____

CONCLUSION   To summarize, patients who are either terminally ill or who are in an irreversible coma often wish to die. Their care is a financial, physical, and emotional burden for their families. Therefore, families should have the right to ask doctors to turn off life-support machines or to remove feeding tubes.

EXERCISE 2
Summarizing an Essay

Write a one-paragraph summary of the model essay "The Right To Die" on pages 169–170.

Writing Assignment

Choose one of the topics in the Try It Out! exercise on page 172 and write an opinion essay. Follow the steps in the writing process.

Step 1 Prewriting

Take a survey and interview your classmates, friends, and/or family in order to gather statistics and quotations.

A. Think of questions that will give you useful quotations and statistics. For example, imagine that your topic is video games. You could ask questions such as these:

- Do you agree or disagree with this statement: "Video games are a bad influence on young people"?
- Why do you think video games are a bad/good influence on young people?
- How many hours do you/your children play video games each day?
- What games do you/your children play?
- Are there young children in your house?
- Are the young children allowed to play any video game or only certain ones?
- How many hours a day do your children spend on schoolwork? How many hours a day do they play outside?

B. Write your questions on a piece of paper. If possible, make one copy for each classmate.
C. Give each classmate a copy of your questions and ask him or her to complete it. If you wish and if your instructor permits, interview friends and family to get more information. Be sure to write down their answers.
D. Compile the answers to develop useful statistics for your paper.
E. Select one or two quotations that support each reason.
F. Save this information to use when you write your essay.

Step 2 Organize the ideas by making an outline.

Use an outline form similar to the following, changing it as necessary to fit your ideas.

Title: _____

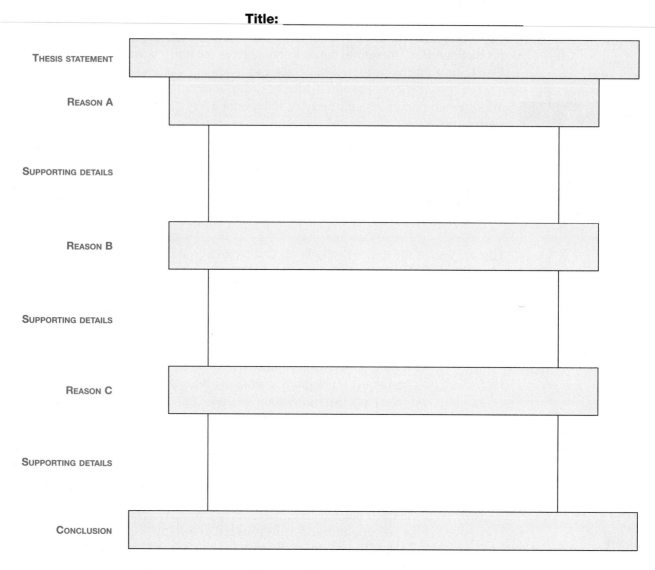

THESIS STATEMENT

REASON A

SUPPORTING DETAILS

REASON B

SUPPORTING DETAILS

REASON C

SUPPORTING DETAILS

CONCLUSION

Step 3 Write the rough draft. Write ROUGH DRAFT at the top of your paper.

Step 4 Polish the rough draft.

- Exchange papers with a classmate and ask him or her to check your rough draft using Peer-Editing Worksheet 10 on page 216. Then discuss the completed worksheet and decide what changes you should make. Write a second draft.
- Use Self-Editing Worksheet 10 on page 217 to check your second draft for grammar, punctuation, and sentence structure.

Step 5 Write a final copy. Hand in your rough draft, your second draft, your final copy, and the page containing the two editing worksheets. Your teacher may also ask you to hand in your prewriting paper.

A Journal Writing[1]

When you learned to speak your first language, you didn't immediately start talking in long, grammatically correct sentences. Instead, you listened and experimented with words and phrases in a nonthreatening environment. By constant repetition, trial, and many errors, you expanded your vocabulary and started to speak in perfect sentences until, by the time you started school, you were fluent in the spoken language.

To acquire a level of fluency in written language you need to experiment with writing words, phrases, and sentences in a nonthreatening environment. Journal writing gives you this opportunity and is, therefore, an important tool for acquiring written fluency.

How Journal Writing Can Help You

1. You improve your writing by writing. In journals, quantity is more important than quality. Writing every day will help you become fluent.

2. You choose the topics. In your journal, you can write about topics that are interesting and relevant to your life. You are practicing expressing your ideas and feelings in your journals.

3. Your journals can help you develop ideas that you can later use in your paragraphs or essays.

4. Writing a journal can be very enjoyable. You don't have to worry about using a dictionary or checking your grammar or organization, and you don't have to write several drafts. You just concentrate on the content.

5. Journal writing helps you develop the language you need in your everyday life. If you are having problems with your landlord or at work, writing about it can help you develop the language you need to solve your problems.

---

[1]This section was adapted from material written by instructor Caroline Gibbs of City College of San Francisco. Used with permission.

How to Start

1. Buy an 8½-inch by 11-inch spiral notebook.

2. Each time you write in your journal, put the date, the time you start, and the time you stop at the top of the page.

3. Don't skip lines. Don't spend a long time thinking or worrying about what you are going to write; just start writing.

4. Write for at least an hour a week. You may write for ten minutes each day or for twenty minutes three times a week. Remember that the more effort you put into your journal, the more your writing will progress.

5. Don't worry about making spelling or other mistakes. Concentrate on your ideas rather than an error-free journal.

6. Try to practice the grammar and new vocabulary or idioms you are learning in class.

7. Write about your daily life, your problems, your feelings, or your opinions. In fact, write about anything that interests you.

8. Your journal will not be shared with other members of the class; only your teacher will be your audience.

9. Your instructor will collect your journals regularly, every week or two, to check that you are doing them, to offer advice on your writing, or to respond to your writing. He/she will *not* correct your grammar or spelling, although he/she may point out recurring errors.

10. If you can't think of a topic to write about or if your instructor prefers, you may brainstorm a list of topics at the beginning of the semester or choose from the following topics.

Journal Writing Topic Suggestions

1. How your life has changed since you came to the United States

2. A special skill you have

3. A hobby

4. Learning to play a sport

5. Your favorite sport to play or watch

6. An accident

7. Being on time

8. The people you live with

9. American customs you like/dislike

10. An important story in the news

11. The working student

12. A big mistake you once made

13. Using e-mail

14. Cell phones

15. Teenagers

16. The right age to get married

17. A good friend

18. Shopping

19. Your last day in your country

20. Your first day in the United States

21. Discrimination

22. Your favorite food

23. The best car to own

24. Smoking in public places

25. A movie star or singer you like

26. A belief you have or used to have

27. A story from your childhood

28. A favorite possession

29. Music that is special to you

30. A special gift you have given or received

31. A special day or event in your life

32. Your worst habit

33. A frightening experience

Correction Symbols

Symbol	Meaning	Example of Error	Corrected Sentence
p	punctuation	I live^p, and go to school here^p	I live and go to school here.
∧	missing word	I ^{am} working in a restaurant. ∧	I am working in a restaurant.
cap	capitalization	It is located at ^{cap}main and ^{cap}baker ^{cap}streets in the ^{cap}City.	It is located at Main and Baker Streets in the city.
vt	verb tense	I never ^{vt}work as a cashier until I ^{vt}get a job there.	I had never worked as a cashier until I got a job there.
s/v agr	subject-verb agreement	The manager ^{s/v agr}work hard. There ^{s/v agr}is five employees.	The manager works hard. There are five employees.
pron agr	pronoun agreement	Everyone works hard at ^{pron agr}their jobs.	All the employees work hard at their jobs.
⌣	connect to make one sentence	We work together. So we have become friends.	We work together, so we have become friends.
sp	spelling	The ^{sp}maneger is a woman.	The manager is a woman.
sing/pl	singular or plural	She treats her employees like ^{sing/pl}slave.	She treats her employees like slaves.
✕	unnecessary word	My boss ~~she~~ watches everyone all the time.	My boss watches everyone all the time.
wf	wrong word form	Her voice is ^{wf}irritated.	Her voice is irritating.

Symbol	Meaning	Example of Error	Corrected Sentence
ww	wrong word	The food is delicious. *ww* <u>Besides</u>, the restaurant is always crowded.	The food is delicious. Therefore, the restaurant is always crowded.
ref	pronoun reference error	The restaurant's *ref* specialty is fish. <u>They</u> are always fresh.	The restaurant's specialty is fish. It is always fresh.
		The food is delicious. *ref* Therefore, <u>it</u> is always crowded.	The food is delicious. Therefore, the restaurant is always crowded.
wo OR ∼	wrong word order	Friday always is our busiest night.	Friday is always our busiest night.
ro	run-on sentence	*ro* [Lily was fired she is upset.]	
cs	comma splice	*cs* [Lily was fired, she is upset.]	Lily was fired, so she is upset.
frag	fragment	She was fired. *frag* [Because she was always late.]	She was fired because she was always late.
		frag [Is open from 6:00 p.m. until the last customer leaves.]	The restaurant is open from 6:00 p.m. until the last customer leaves.
		frag [The employees on time and work hard.]	The employees are on time and work hard.
not //	not parallel	Most of our regular *not //* customers are <u>friendly</u> <u>and generous tippers</u>.	Most of our regular customers are friendly and tip generously.

Symbol	Meaning	Example of Error	Corrected Sentence
prep	preposition	We start serving prep dinner ⌄6:00 p.m.	We start serving dinner at 6:00 p.m.
conj	conjunction	Garlic shrimp, fried conj clams, ⌄broiled lobster are the most popular dishes.	Garlic shrimp, fried clams, and broiled lobster are the most popular dishes.
art	article	Diners in the United art States expect ⌄glass of water when they first sit down.	Diners in the United States expect a glass of water when they first sit down.
Ⓣ	add a transition	The new employee Ⓣ was careless. She frequently spilled coffee on the table.	The new employee was careless. For example, she frequently spilled coffee on the table.
¶	start a new paragraph		
nfs/nmp	needs further support/needs more proof. You need to add some specific details (examples, facts, quotations) to support your points.		

Summary of Punctuation Rules

The following chart summarizes punctuation rules covered in this book.

Use Commas	Example
1. To separate items in a series of three or more items	I'm taking Spanish, English, physics, and economics this semester. The teacher will read your paragraph, make comments on it, and return it to you.
2. Before a coordinating conjunction in a compound sentence	We are bringing sandwiches, and Tom is bringing soft drinks to the picnic. We don't need to bring raincoats, for the sun is shining brightly.
3. After a dependent clause that comes before an independent clause in a complex sentence (Don't use a comma when the dependent clause follows the independent clause.)	Because the sun is shining brightly, we don't need to bring raincoats. As soon as we arrived at the park, the men started playing soccer. (The men played soccer while the women watched.)
4. To separate extra-information adjective clauses from the rest of the sentence	The Nile, which is the longest river in the world, is 4,160 miles long.
5. To separate extra-information appositives from the rest of the sentence	The Amazon, the second longest river, is 4,000 miles long.
6. After most transition signals at the beginning of a sentence	Finally, we arrived at our hotel. However, our rooms were not ready. After an hour, we left to find a place to eat. Across the street, we found a small cafe.
7. To separate sentence connectors that appear in the middle of an independent clause.	Our rooms, however, were not ready. Lions, for example, can outrun all but three animals.

188 Appendix C | Summary of Punctuation Rules

Use Apostrophes	Example
1. To replace missing letters in contractions	She's always cheerful. They didn't answer the telephone.
2. With *s* to show possession with nouns and indefinite pronouns	He found a girl's jacket in the hall. He walked into the girls' gymnasium by mistake. He found someone's jacket in the hall.
3. With *s* to form the plural of numbers and letters.	The ice skater received three 10's and two 9.5's for her performance. The teacher gave all A's and B's last semester.

Use Quotation Marks	Example
To separate the exact words someone says or writes from a reporting phrase	She said, "I'll miss you." "I'll write you every day," she promised. "I'll think about you every day," she continued, "and I'll dream about you every night."

APPENDIX

D Kinds of Sentences and Master List of Connecting Words

Kinds of Sentences

Simple sentence = one independent clause

Spring has arrived!

The flowers are blooming.

The sun is shining brightly.

People are walking and jogging in the park.

Compound sentence = two independent clauses

The sun is shining, and there are no clouds in the sky.

It was a beautiful day, so we decided to go to the skateboard park.

Complex sentence = one independent clause + one (or more) dependent clauses

As soon as we arrived, we put on our rollerblades.

Alex broke his arm because he wasn't careful.

Connecting Words

Coordinating Conjunctions

Coordinating conjunctions connect grammatically equal parts of a sentence. The parts can be words, phrases, or clauses.

Coordinating Conjunction	Use	Example
and	Connects equal similar ideas.	John likes to fish **and** hunt. John likes to fish, **and** he often goes fishing with friends.
but	Connects equal different ideas.	I like to eat fish **but** not to catch them. John likes to catch fish, **but** he doesn't like to eat them.

(continued on next page)

Coordinating Conjunction	Use	Example
or	Connects two equal choices.	Do you prefer coffee **or** tea? They can register for classes online, **or** they can register by mail.
so	Connects a result to a reason.	I did not eat breakfast this morning, **so** I am a little hungry.
yet	Connects equal contrasting ideas.	It is sunny **yet** cold. John fished all day, **yet** he didn't get one bite.
for	Connects a reason to a result.	I am a little hungry, **for** I didn't eat breakfast this morning.
nor	Connects two negative sentences.	She does not eat meat, **nor** does she drink milk.

Subordinating Conjunctions

A subordinating conjunction (or subordinator) is the first word in a dependent clause. Common subordinators include the following.

Subordinating Conjunctions	
To tell a time	
after	He goes to school **after** he finishes work.
as	Several overcrowded busses passed **as** they were waiting.
as soon as	She felt better **as soon as** she took the medicine.
before	**Before** you apply to college, you have to take an entrance exam.
since	It has been a year **since** I left home.
until	We can't leave the room **until** everyone finishes the test.
when	**When** you start college, you sometimes have to take a placement test.
whenever	**Whenever** I don't sleep well, I feel sick the next day.
while	Several overcrowded busses passed **while** we were waiting.
To give a reason	
because	Jack excels at sports **because** he trains hard.
since	**Since** she works out daily, Jill is in great condition.
as	**As** they want to compete in a marathon, they run every day.

To tell where	
where	I can never remember **where** I put my house keys.
wherever	A baby animal follows its mother **wherever** she goes.
To make a contrast	
although	I love my brother **although** we disagree about almost everything.
even though	I love my brother **even though** we disagree about almost everything.
though	I love my brother **though** we disagree about almost everything.
while	My brother likes classical music, **while** I prefer hard rock.
whereas	He dresses conservatively, **whereas** I like to be a little shocking.

Relative Pronouns

Subordinating words for adjective clauses are called relative pronouns.

Relative Pronouns	
To refer to people	
who, whom, that (informal)	People **who** live in glass houses should not throw stones. My parents did not approve of the man **whom** my sister married. He's a man **that** everyone in our town respects.
To refer to animals and things	
which	My new computer, **which** I bought yesterday, stopped working today.
that	Yesterday I received an e-mail **that** I did not understand.
To refer to a time	
when	Thanksgiving is a time **when** families travel great distances to be together.

Master Chart of Transition Signals

The following chart lists the transition signals used in this book.

Sentence Connectors	Coordinating Conjunctions	Subordinating Conjunctions	Others
To list ideas in time order			
First, Second, First of all, Next, Meanwhile, After that, Finally, Now Soon Then		after as as soon as before since until when whenever while	At last, At 12:00, After a while, Before beginning the lesson, In the morning, The next day, The first step . . . The second step . . . After five minutes,
To list ideas in logical division of ideas order			
First, Second, etc. First of all, Furthermore, Also, In addition, Moreover,	and		A second (reason, kind, advantage, etc.) . . . An additional (reason, kind, advantage, etc.) . . . The final (reason, kind, advantage, etc.) . . .
To add a similar idea			
Similarly, Likewise, Also, Furthermore, In addition, Moreover,	and (Paired conjunctions) both . . . and not only . . . but also		
To make a comparison			
Similarly, Likewise, Also, too	and . . . (too) (Paired conjunctions) both . . . and not only . . . but also	(just) as	similar (to) equal (to) equally the same (as) (just) like

To add an opposite idea			
On the other hand, However,	but yet		

To make a contrast			
On the other hand, However, In contrast,	but yet	while whereas although though even though	different (from) differently unlike differ (from) (in)

To give an example			
For example, For instance,			such as . . . An example of . . .

To give a reason			
	for	because since as	because of (+ noun)

To give a result			
Therefore, Thus, Consequently, As a result,	so		

To add a conclusion			

All in all,
For these reasons,
In brief,
In conclusion,
Indeed,
In short,
In summary,
To conclude,
To summarize,
To sum up,
			It is clear that . . .
			These examples
			  show that . . .
			You can see that . . .
			You can see from
			  these examples
			  that . . .

Peer-Editing and Self-Editing Worksheets; Scoring Rubrics

Peer-editing and Self-editing worksheets are designed to help you become a better writer. Your instructor may choose to assign the peer-editing worksheet, the self-editing worksheet, or both.

Peer Editing

Peer editing is an interactive process of reading and commenting on a classmate's writing. You will exchange rough drafts with a classmate, read each other's work, and make suggestions for improvement. Use the worksheet for each assignment and answer each question. Write your comments on the worksheet or on your classmate's paper as your instructor directs.

Advice for Peer Editors

1. Your job is to help your classmate write clearly. Focus only on content and organization.
2. If you notice grammar or spelling errors, ignore them. It is not your job to correct your classmate's English.
3. Don't cross out any writing. Underline, draw arrows, circle things, but don't cross out anything.
4. Make your first comment a positive one. Find something good to say.
5. If possible, use a colored pencil or ink.
6. The writer may not always agree with you. Discuss your different opinions, but don't argue, and don't hurt your classmate's feelings.

Self-Editing

Becoming a better writer requires that you learn to edit your own work. Self-editing involves not just checking for spelling and grammar errors. It also means looking at your writing as a writing teacher does. The self-editing worksheets contain questions about specific elements that your teacher hopes to find in your paragraph or essay— a strong thesis statement, clear topic sentences, specific supporting details, coherence, an effective conclusion, and so on. By answering the worksheet questions thoughtfully, you can learn to recognize the strengths and weaknesses in your rhetorical skills as well as to spot recurring errors in grammar, punctuation, and sentence structure.

Here are some polite ways to suggest changes.

Do you think _____ is important/necessary/relevant?
I don't quite understand your meaning here.
Could you please explain this point a little more?
I think an example would help here.
This part seems confusing.
I think this part should go at the end/at the beginning/after XYZ.
Maybe you don't need this word/sentence/part.

Scoring Rubrics

When grading papers, writing teachers sometimes assign points for each writing skill. They often use a rubric such as the ones on pages 196 and 197. The first rubric is for scoring paragraphs; the second one is for scoring essays. In each rubric, the left column shows the maximum number of points possible for each item.

Teachers may duplicate these forms to use when scoring students' work.

Scoring Rubric: Paragraphs

	Maximum Score	Actual Score
Format—5 points		
There is a title.	1	_____
The title is centered.	1	_____
The first line is indented.	1	_____
There are margins on both sides.	1	_____
The paragraph is double-spaced.	1	_____
Total	5	
Punctuation and Mechanics—5 points		
There is a period after every sentence.	1	_____
Capital letters are used correctly.	1	_____
The spelling is correct.	1	_____
Commas are used correctly.	2	_____
Total	5	
Content—20 points		
The paragraph fits the assignment.	5	_____
The paragraph is interesting to read.	5	_____
The paragraph shows that the writer used care and thought.	10	_____
Total	20	
Organization—35 points		
The paragraph begins with a topic sentence that has both a topic and a controlling idea.	10	_____
The paragraph contains several specific and factual supporting sentences that explain or prove the topic sentence, including at least one example.	20	_____
The paragraph ends with an appropriate concluding sentence.	5	_____
Total	35	
Grammar and Sentence Structure—35 points		
Estimate a grammar and sentence structure score.	35	
Grand Total	100	

Scoring Rubric: Essays

	Maximum Score	Actual Score
Format—5 points Title centered (2), first line of each paragraph indented (1), margins left on both sides (1), text double-spaced (1)		
Total	5	
Punctuation and Mechanics—5 points Periods, commas, apostrophes, and quotation marks (3), capital letters (1), spelling (1)		
Total	5	
Content—20 points		
The essay fulfills the requirements of the assignment.	5	———
The essay is interesting.	5	———
The essay shows that the writer used care and thought.	10	———
Total	20	
Organization—45 points		
The essay follows the outline, and it has an introduction, a body, and a conclusion.	5	———
Introductory Paragraph: The introductory paragraph begins with several general sentences and ends with a thesis statement.	5	———
Body		
Each paragraph of the body discusses a new point and begins with a clear topic sentence.	5	———
Each paragraph has specific supporting material: facts, examples, quotations, paraphrased or summarized information, and so on.	10	———
Each paragraph has unity.	5	———
Each paragraph has coherence.	5	———
Transitions are used to link paragraphs.	5	———
Concluding Paragraph: The concluding paragraph summarizes the main points or paraphrases the thesis statement, begins with a conclusion signal, and leaves the reader with the writer's final thoughts on the topic.	5	———
Total	45	
Grammar and Sentence Structure—25 points		
Estimate a grammar and sentence structure score.	25	
Grand Total	100	

Peer Editor: _____ Date: _____

If your instructor approves, write your comments directly on the paper you are editing. If your instructor prefers that you not write on your classmate's paper, use this form, and when the directions tell you to underline or circle, copy the item on the form instead.

1. Is the paragraph interesting? ☐ **yes** ☐ **no**

   Was the person written about already familiar to you, ☐ **already familiar**
   or did you learn about this person from reading the paragraph? ☐ **new to me**

   Write a comment about a part that is especially interesting to you.

   _____

   _____

2. Do you understand everything? ☐ **yes** ☐ **no**

   Circle or underline any part that you do not understand, and write a comment about it.

   _____

   _____

3. How many sentences are there in the paragraph? **number** _____

   Would you like more information about anything? ☐ **yes** ☐ **no**

   If your answer is yes, write down what you would like to know more about.

   _____

   _____

4. Check the format (title, indenting, spacing, margins, etc.). Make a note about anything that seems incorrect to you.

   _____

   _____

5. In your opinion, what is the best feature of this paragraph? In other words, what is this writer's best writing skill?

   _____

   _____

Self-Editing Worksheet 1
Chapter 1: Paragraph Format

Writer: _____ Date: _____

Format

My paragraph has a title.	☐ **yes**	☐ **no**
The title is centered.	☐ **yes**	☐ **no**
The first line is indented.	☐ **yes**	☐ **no**
There are margins on both sides of the page.	☐ **yes**	☐ **no**
My paragraph is double-spaced.	☐ **yes**	☐ **no**

Content and Organization

My paragraph fits the assignment.	☐ **yes**	☐ **no**
I did not copy any sentences from another book or online source.	☐ **yes**	☐ **no**
If I used information from another book, I rewrote the information in my own words.	☐ **yes**	☐ **no**

Punctuation, Capitalization, and Spelling

I put a period after every sentence.	☐ **yes**	☐ **no**
I used capital letters correctly.	☐ **yes**	☐ **no**
I checked my spelling.	☐ **yes**	☐ **no**

Grammar and Sentence Structure

I checked my paragraph for subject-verb agreement.	☐ **yes**	☐ **no**
I checked my paragraph for fragments.	☐ **yes**	☐ **no**

Every student has his or her own personal grammar trouble spots. Some students battle with verb tenses. For others, articles are the main enemy. Some find it hard to know where to put periods.

On the lines below, add items that you know are problems for you. Then, throughout the term, work on eliminating these errors. Delete items that you have mastered and add new ones that you become aware of.

Errors to check for include verb tenses, subject-verb agreement, articles, pronoun agreement, sentence fragments, and run-on sentences.

Personal Grammar Trouble Spots

Number found and corrected

I checked my paragraph for _____ errors. _____
(verb tense, article, etc.)

I checked my paragraph for _____ errors. _____

I checked my paragraph for _____ errors. _____

Peer Editor: _____ Date: _____

1. Is the paragraph interesting? ☐ **yes** ☐ **no**

   Write a comment about a part that is especially interesting to you.

   _____

   _____

2. Do you understand everything? ☐ **yes** ☐ **no**

   Circle or underline any part that you do not understand, and write a comment about it.

   _____

   _____

3. Copy the topic sentence here, and circle the topic and underline the controlling idea.

   _____

   _____

4. How many supporting sentences are there in the paragraph? **number** _____

   Is there at least one example for every supporting point? ☐ **yes** ☐ **no**

5. Would you like more information about anything? ☐ **yes** ☐ **no**

   If your answer is yes, write down what you would like to know more about.

   _____

   _____

6. If the paragraph has a concluding sentence, copy it here and circle the end-of-paragraph signal (if there is one).

   _____

   _____

7. In your opinion, what is the best feature of this paragraph? In other words, what is this writer's best writing skill?

   _____

   _____

Self-Editing Worksheet 2
Chapter 2: Paragraph Structure

Writer: _____ Date: _____

Format

My paragraph has a title.	☐ yes	☐ no
The title is centered.	☐ yes	☐ no
The first line is indented.	☐ yes	☐ no
There are margins on both sides of the page.	☐ yes	☐ no
The paragraph is double-spaced.	☐ yes	☐ no

Content and Organization

My paragraph fits the assignment.	☐ yes	☐ no
My paragraph has a topic sentence.	☐ yes	☐ no
The topic sentence has both a topic and a controlling idea.	☐ yes	☐ no
My paragraph contains several supporting points and at least one example for each point.	☐ yes	☐ no

I wrote _____ supporting sentences.
  (number)

My paragraph ends with an appropriate concluding sentence.	☐ yes	☐ no

Punctuation, Capitalization, and Spelling

I put a period after every sentence.	☐ yes	☐ no
I used capital letters correctly.	☐ yes	☐ no
I checked my spelling.	☐ yes	☐ no

Grammar and Sentence Structure

I wrote _____ compound sentences and punctuated them correctly. ☐ yes ☐ no
  (number)

I checked my paragraph for subject-verb agreement.	☐ yes	☐ no
I checked my paragraph for fragments.	☐ yes	☐ no

Personal Grammar Trouble Spots

Number found and corrected

I checked my paragraph for _____ errors.   _____
                          (verb tense, article, etc.)

I checked my paragraph for _____ errors.   _____

I checked my paragraph for _____ errors.   _____

Peer Editor: _____ Date: _____

1. Is the paragraph interesting?   ☐ **yes**   ☐ **no**

Write a comment about a part that is especially interesting to you.

_____

_____

2. Do you understand everything?   ☐ **yes**   ☐ **no**

Circle or underline any part that you do not understand, and write a comment about it.

_____

_____

3. Would you like more information about anything?   ☐ **yes**   ☐ **no**

If your answer is yes, write down what you would like to know more about.

_____

_____

4. Does the paragraph begin with a topic sentence?   ☐ **yes**   ☐ **no**

Copy the topic sentence: _____

_____

5. Does the writer use time order to organize the paragraph?   ☐ **yes**   ☐ **no**

What time order words and phrases can you find? Copy them here: _____

_____

Check to make sure commas are used correctly after time words and phrases. Make a note about any missing commas.

_____

_____

6. Look for compound sentences. Check to make sure each compound sentence has a comma before the conjunction. Make a note about any missing commas.

_____

_____

7. In your opinion, what is the best feature of this paragraph? In other words, what is this writer's best writing skill?

_____

_____

Writer: _____   Date: _____

Format

My paragraph is in the correct format (centered title, first line
indented, margins on both sides, double-spaced).   ☐ **yes**   ☐ **no**

Content and Organization

My paragraph fits the assignment. I used time order to tell about
an important or memorable event in my life.   ☐ **yes**   ☐ **no**

I introduced some/most/all events with time order words or phrases.
(Underline *some, most,* or *all*.)   ☐ **yes**   ☐ **no**

Punctuation, Capitalization, and Spelling

I put a period after every sentence.   ☐ **yes**   ☐ **no**

I put a comma in my compound sentences.   ☐ **yes**   ☐ **no**

I used commas correctly after time signal words and phrases.   ☐ **yes**   ☐ **no**

I used capital letters correctly.   ☐ **yes**   ☐ **no**

I checked my spelling.   ☐ **yes**   ☐ **no**

Grammar and Sentence Structure

I wrote _____ compound sentences and punctuated them correctly.   ☐ **yes**   ☐ **no**
    (number)

I checked my paragraph for subject-verb agreement.   ☐ **yes**   ☐ **no**

I checked my paragraph for fragments.   ☐ **yes**   ☐ **no**

Personal Grammar Trouble Spots

**Number found
and corrected**

I checked my paragraph for _____ errors.   _____
                          (verb tense, article, etc.)

I checked my paragraph for _____ errors.   _____

I checked my paragraph for _____ errors.   _____

Peer Editor: _____ Date: _____

1. What place does the writer describe in the paragraph?

   _____

   _____

2. Does the paragraph begin with a topic sentence?   ☐ **yes**   ☐ **no**

   Copy the topic sentence here: _____

   _____

3. Does the writer use spatial order to organize the paragraph?   ☐ **yes**   ☐ **no**

   What is the order (front to back, bottom to top, near to far, right to left, etc.)?

   _____

   What spatial order words and phrases can you find? Copy them here: _____

   _____

4. Does the writer give specific details to help you "see" the place he or she describes? Write three of the details:

   a. _____

   b. _____

   c. _____

5. Are there any sentences that are off the topic? If your answer is yes, write them here (or mark them on the paragraph if your teacher allows you to write on other students' work).

   _____

   _____

6. Look for compound sentences. Check to make sure each compound sentence has a comma before the coordinating conjunction. Make a note about any missing commas.

   _____

   _____

7. In your opinion, what is the best feature of this paragraph? In other words, what is this writer's best writing skill?

   _____

   _____

Writer: _____   Date: _____

Format

My paragraph is in the correct format (centered title, first line
  indented, margins on both sides, double-spaced).   ☐ **yes**   ☐ **no**

Content and Organization

My paragraph fits the assignment. I used spatial order to describe
  a place.   ☐ **yes**   ☐ **no**

I used _____ spatial order to organize my description.
  (near-to-far, left-to-right, top-to-bottom, etc.)

I used the following spatial order expressions:

_____

_____

My paragraph has a topic sentence, several supporting sentences,
  and a concluding sentence.   ☐ **yes**   ☐ **no**

My paragraph has unity. No sentences are off the topic.   ☐ **yes**   ☐ **no**

Punctuation, Capitalization, and Spelling

I put a period after every sentence.   ☐ **yes**   ☐ **no**

I put a comma in my compound sentences.   ☐ **yes**   ☐ **no**

I used capital letters correctly.   ☐ **yes**   ☐ **no**

I checked my spelling.   ☐ **yes**   ☐ **no**

Grammar and Sentence Structure

I checked my paragraph for fragments.   ☐ **yes**   ☐ **no**

I varied my sentence structure by writing a prepositional phrase at   ☐ **yes**   ☐ **no**
  the beginning of at least one sentence (copy that sentence here): _____

_____

I wrote _____ compound sentences.
  (number)

Personal Grammar Trouble Spots

**Number found
and corrected**

I checked my paragraph for _____ errors.   _____
                              (verb tense, article, etc.)

I checked my paragraph for _____ errors.   _____

I checked my paragraph for _____ errors.   _____

Peer Editor: _____ Date: _____

1. Is the paragraph interesting?   ☐ yes   ☐ no

   Write a comment about a part that is especially interesting to you.

   _____

   _____

2. Do you understand everything?   ☐ yes   ☐ no

   Circle or underline any part that you do not understand, and write a comment about it.

   _____

   _____

3. Copy the topic sentence here, and circle the topic and underline the controlling idea.

   _____

4. How many supporting points are there in the paragraph?   number _____

   Is each point introduced by a transition signal?   ☐ yes   ☐ no

   Is there at least one example for every supporting point?   ☐ yes   ☐ no

5. Would you like more information about anything?   ☐ yes   ☐ no

   If your answer is yes, write down what you would like to know more about.

   _____

   _____

6. How many transition signals can you find?   number _____

   Are there too many or just about the right number of transition signals?

   _____

7. In your opinion, what is the best feature of this paragraph? In other words, what is this writer's best writing skill?

   _____

   _____

Self-Editing Worksheet 5
Chapter 5: Logical Division of Ideas

Writer: _____ Date: _____

Format

My paragraph is in the correct format (centered title, first line
indented, margins on both sides, double-spaced).   ☐ **yes**   ☐ **no**

Content and Organization

My paragraph fits the assignment. I use logical division of ideas
to organize my ideas.   ☐ **yes**   ☐ **no**

My paragraph begins with a topic sentence that contains both a topic
and a controlling idea.   ☐ **yes**   ☐ **no**

My paragraph contains several supporting points.   ☐ **yes**   ☐ **no**

    I introduce each new point with a transition signal.   ☐ **yes**   ☐ **no**

    I use at least one example for each point.   ☐ **yes**   ☐ **no**

My paragraph ends with an appropriate concluding sentence.   ☐ **yes**   ☐ **no**

My paragraph has unity.   ☐ **yes**   ☐ **no**

My paragraph has coherence.   ☐ **yes**   ☐ **no**

    I use nouns and pronouns consistently.   ☐ **yes**   ☐ **no**

    I use transition signals where they are appropriate. These are some   ☐ **yes**   ☐ **no**
    of the transition signals in my paragraph: _____

_____

_____

Punctuation, Capitalization, and Spelling

I checked my paragraph for correct punctuation, capitalization,
and spelling.   ☐ **yes**   ☐ **no**

Grammar and Sentence Structure

I wrote both simple and compound sentences and punctuated
them correctly.   ☐ **yes**   ☐ **no**

I checked my paragraph for fragments.   ☐ **yes**   ☐ **no**

I checked my paragraph for run-ons and comma splices.   ☐ **yes**   ☐ **no**

Personal Grammar Trouble Spots

**Number found
and corrected**

I checked my paragraph for _____ errors.   _____
                         (verb tense, article, etc.)

I checked my paragraph for _____ errors.   _____

I checked my paragraph for _____ errors.   _____

Peer Editor: _____ Date: _____

1. Is the process explained in the paragraph interesting?   ☐ **yes**   ☐ **no**

   Write a comment about a part that is especially interesting to you.

   _____

   _____

2. Do you understand every step?   ☐ **yes**   ☐ **no**

   Circle or underline any step that you do not understand, and write a comment about it.

   _____

   _____

3. Copy the topic sentence here, and circle the topic and underline the words that tell you that this is a process paragraph.

   _____

   _____

4. How many steps are there?   **number** _____

   Is each step introduced by a time order signal?   ☐ **yes**   ☐ **no**

5. Would you like more information about any step?   ☐ **yes**   ☐ **no**

   If your answer is yes, write down what you would like to know more about.

   _____

   _____

6. How many transition signals can you find?   **number** _____

   Are there too many or just about the right number of transition signals?

   _____

7. Would you be able to do the process explained in this paragraph? Why or why not?

   _____

   _____

Writer: _____   Date: _____

Format

My paragraph is in the correct format (centered title, first line indented,
   margins on both sides, double-spaced). ☐ **yes** ☐ **no**

Content and Organization

My paragraph fits the assignment. I use time order to explain a process. ☐ **yes** ☐ **no**

My paragraph begins with a topic sentence that tells my reader
   to look for a series of steps. ☐ **yes** ☐ **no**

My paragraph explains each step in the process. ☐ **yes** ☐ **no**

   I introduce each new step with a transition signal. ☐ **yes** ☐ **no**

My paragraph ends with a concluding sentence that either is the last
   step in the process or gives the results of the process. ☐ **yes** ☐ **no**

My paragraph has unity. ☐ **yes** ☐ **no**

My paragraph has coherence. ☐ **yes** ☐ **no**

   I use nouns and pronouns consistently. ☐ **yes** ☐ **no**

   I use transition signals where they are appropriate. These are some ☐ **yes** ☐ **no**
     of the transition signals in my paragraph: _____

_____

_____

Punctuation, Capitalization, and Spelling

I checked my paragraph for correct punctuation, capitalization,
   and spelling. ☐ **yes** ☐ **no**

Grammar and Sentence Structure

I wrote _____ complex sentences and punctuated them correctly.
    (number)

I checked my paragraph for fragments, run-ons, and comma splices. ☐ **yes** ☐ **no**

Personal Grammar Trouble Spots

**Number found
and corrected**

I checked my paragraph for _____ errors. _____
         (verb tense, article, etc.)

I checked my paragraph for _____ errors. _____

I checked my paragraph for _____ errors. _____

Peer Editor: _____ Date: _____

1. Is the word, custom, or holiday explained in the paragraph interesting?   ☐ **yes**   ☐ **no**

   Write a comment about a part that is especially interesting to you.

   _____

   _____

2. Do you understand everything?   ☐ **yes**   ☐ **no**

   Circle or underline anything that you do not understand, and write a comment about it.

   _____

   _____

3. Copy the topic sentence here, and circle the topic, underline the category or group, and double-underline the distinguishing characteristic.

   _____

   _____

4. How many supporting sentences are there?   **number** _____

5. Would you like more information about anything?   ☐ **yes**   ☐ **no**

   If your answer is yes, write down what you would like to know more about.

   _____

   _____

6. How many adjective clauses and appositives can you find?   **number** _____

   Copy one of them here. _____

   _____

7. What do you like best about this paragraph? In other words, what is this writer's best writing skill?

   _____

   _____

Self-Editing Worksheet 7
Chapter 7: Definition

Writer: _____ Date: _____

Format

My paragraph is in the correct format (centered title, first line
  indented, margins on both sides, double-spaced). ☐ **yes** ☐ **no**

Content and Organization

My paragraph fits the assignment. I wrote a definition of a word,
  custom, or holiday. ☐ **yes** ☐ **no**

My paragraph begins with a topic sentence that names the topic,
  the category or group, and distinguishing characteristic. ☐ **yes** ☐ **no**

My supporting sentences explain my topic completely. ☐ **yes** ☐ **no**

My paragraph ends with a concluding sentence. ☐ **yes** ☐ **no**

My paragraph has unity. ☐ **yes** ☐ **no**

My paragraph has coherence. ☐ **yes** ☐ **no**

　　I use nouns and pronouns consistently. ☐ **yes** ☐ **no**

　　I use the following transition signals where they are appropriate: ☐ **yes** ☐ **no**

_____

_____

_____

Punctuation, Capitalization, and Spelling

I checked my paragraph for correct punctuation, capitalization,
  and spelling. ☐ **yes** ☐ **no**

Grammar and Sentence Structure

I used at least one adjective clause and one appositive in my paragraph
  and punctuated them correctly. ☐ **yes** ☐ **no**

I checked my paragraph for fragments, run-ons, and comma splices. ☐ **yes** ☐ **no**

Personal Grammar Trouble Spots

**Number found
and corrected**

I checked my paragraph for _____ errors. _____
  (verb tense, article, etc.)

I checked my paragraph for _____ errors. _____

I checked my paragraph for _____ errors. _____

Peer Editor: _____ Date: _____

1. What two items does the writer compare or contrast in the paragraph?

   _____

2. Do you understand everything?   ☐ **yes**   ☐ **no**

   Circle or underline any step that you do not understand, and write a comment about it.

   _____

   _____

3. Copy the topic sentence. Circle the topic and underline the words that tell you that this is a comparison/contrast paragraph.

   _____

   _____

4. On what points does the writer compare or contrast the items? List them.

   _____

   _____

5. Is each new point introduced by a transition signal?   ☐ **yes**   ☐ **no**

6. Would you like more information about anything?   ☐ **yes**   ☐ **no**

   If your answer is yes, write down what you would like to know more about.

   _____

   _____

7. How many comparison/contrast signals can you find?   **number** _____

   Are there too many or just about the right number of signals?

   _____

8. In your opinion, what is the best feature of this paragraph? In other words, what is this writer's best writing skill?

   _____

   _____

Writer: _____ Date: _____

Format

My paragraph is in the correct format (centered title, first line
   indented, margins on both sides, double-spaced).   ☐ yes   ☐ no

Content and Organization

My paragraph fits the assignment. I compare or contrast two people,
   places, ideas, or cultures.   ☐ yes   ☐ no

   I compare them on _____ points. (*Write a number.*)

My paragraph begins with a topic sentence that tells my reader
   to look for a comparison or contrast.   ☐ yes   ☐ no

My paragraph is organized in one of these patterns:

   ☐ block pattern   ☐ point-by-point pattern   ☐ yes   ☐ no

I used the following comparison or contrast signals: _____

_____

_____

My paragraph ends with a concluding sentence.   ☐ yes   ☐ no

My paragraph has unity.   ☐ yes   ☐ no

My paragraph has coherence.   ☐ yes   ☐ no

Punctuation, Capitalization, and Spelling

I checked my paragraph for correct punctuation, capitalization,
   and spelling.   ☐ yes   ☐ no

Grammar and Sentence Structure

I varied my sentence structure by writing simple, compound,
   and complex sentences.   ☐ yes   ☐ no

I checked my paragraph for fragments, run-ons, and comma splices.   ☐ yes   ☐ no

Personal Grammar Trouble Spots

**Number found
and corrected**

I checked my paragraph for _____ errors.   _____
            (verb tense, article, etc.)

I checked my paragraph for _____ errors.   _____

I checked my paragraph for _____ errors.   _____

Peer-Editing Worksheet 9
Chapter 9: Essay Organization

Peer Editor: _____ Date: _____

1. Do the first few sentences of the introduction lead you to the thesis statement?   ☐ **yes**   ☐ **no**
   Where is the thesis statement ?
   _____

2. How many paragraphs are there in the body?   **number** _____
   What are the topics of the body paragraphs?
   1. _____   3. _____
   2. _____   4. _____

   (If there are more or fewer paragraphs, add or delete lines.)

3. What kind of supporting details does the writer use in each body paragraph (examples, statistics, facts, etc.)?
   _____

4. Check each paragraph for unity. Is any sentence unnecessary or off the topic?   ☐ **yes**   ☐ **no**
   If your answer is yes, write a comment about it (them).
   _____

5. Check each paragraph for coherence. Does each one flow smoothly from
   beginning to end?   ☐ **yes**   ☐ **no**
   a. What key nouns are repeated? _____
   b. What transition signals can you find? _____
   _____

6. What expressions does the writer use to link paragraphs? If there is none, write *none*. (If there are more or
   fewer paragraphs, add or delete lines.)
   To introduce the first body paragraph: _____
   Between Paragraphs 2 and 3: _____
   Between Paragraphs 3 and 4: _____
   Between Paragraphs 4 and 5: _____
   To introduce the conclusion: _____

7. What kind of conclusion does this essay have—a summary of the main points or a restatement of the
   thesis statement? _____
   Does the writer make a final comment?   ☐ **yes**   ☐ **no**
   What is it? _____
   _____

   Is this an effective ending (one that you will remember)?   ☐ **yes**   ☐ **no**

8. In your opinion, what is the best feature of this essay? In other words, what is this writer's best writing skill?
   _____
   _____

Self-Editing Worksheet 9
Chapter 9: Essay Organization

Writer: _____   Date: _____

Format
My essay is in the correct format (title centered, first line of every paragraph
   indented, margins on both sides, double-spaced).   ☐ yes   ☐ no

Content and Organization
My essay fits the assignment.   ☐ yes   ☐ no

Introduction
I wrote a "funnel introduction."   ☐ yes   ☐ no

The last sentence of my introduction is my thesis statement. (Copy your thesis
   statement.)   ☐ yes   ☐ no

_____

_____

Body
The body has _____ paragraphs. (*Write a number.*)

In each body paragraph, I discuss a different aspect of my main topic.   ☐ yes   ☐ no

Each body paragraph begins with a topic sentence that tells which aspect it will discuss.   ☐ yes   ☐ no

I used supporting details in each paragraph. (*Write the number used in each paragraph.*)   ☐ yes   ☐ no

   Body paragraph 1 _____ Body paragraph 2 _____

   Body paragraph 3 _____ Body paragraph 4 _____

Conclusion
In my conclusion, I (check one)   ☐ summarize my reasons   ☐ repeat my thesis in different words

Unity
Each paragraph discusses only one idea, and there are no sentences that are off the topic.   ☐ yes   ☐ no

Coherence
Each paragraph flows smoothly from beginning to end.   ☐ yes   ☐ no

I repeat key nouns and pronouns.   ☐ yes   ☐ no

I use transition signals to show relationships among ideas.   ☐ yes   ☐ no

I use transition signals to link paragraphs.   ☐ yes   ☐ no

Punctuation, Capitalization, and Spelling
I checked my punctuation, capitalization, and spelling.   ☐ yes   ☐ no

Grammar and Sentence Structure
I varied my sentence structure by writing simple, compound, and complex sentences.   ☐ yes   ☐ no

I checked my paragraph for fragments, comma splices, and run-ons.   ☐ yes   ☐ no

Personal Grammar Trouble Spots

**Number found
and corrected**

I checked my paragraph for _____ errors.   _____
                    (verb tense, article, etc.)

I checked my paragraph for _____ errors.   _____

I checked my paragraph for _____ errors.   _____

Peer Editor: _____ Date: _____

1. Do the first few sentences of the introduction explain the problem or issue?

    _____

    Where is the thesis statement ?

    _____

2. How many paragraphs are there in the body? _____ (*Write a number.*)
    The topics of the body paragraphs are as follows:
    1. _____   3. _____
    2. _____   4. _____

    (If there are more or fewer paragraphs, add or delete lines.)

3. What kind of supporting details does the writer use in each body paragraph?
    Paragraph 1 _____
    Paragraph 2 _____
    Paragraph 3 _____
    Paragraph 4 _____

4. Check each paragraph for unity. Is any sentence unnecessary or off the topic?   ☐ **yes**   ☐ **no**
    If your answer is yes, write a comment about it (them).

    _____

    _____

5. Check each paragraph for coherence. Does each one flow smoothly
    from beginning to end?   ☐ **yes**   ☐ **no**
    a. What key nouns are repeated? _____
    b. What transition signals can you find? _____

    _____

6. What expressions does the writer use to link paragraphs? If there is none, write *none*. (If there are more or
    fewer paragraphs, add or delete lines.)

    To introduce the first body paragraph: _____
    Between Paragraphs 2 and 3: _____
    Between Paragraphs 3 and 4: _____
    Between Paragraphs 4 and 5: _____
    To introduce the conclusion: _____

7. What kind of conclusion does this essay have—a summary of the main points or a restatement of the
    thesis statement? _____

    Does the writer give a final comment?   ☐ **yes**   ☐ **no**
    What is it? _____

    _____

    Is this an effective ending (one that you will remember)?   ☐ **yes**   ☐ **no**

8. In your opinion, what is the best feature of this essay? In other words, what is this writer's best writing skill?

    _____

    _____

Self-Editing Worksheet 10
Chapter 10: Opinion Essay

Writer: _____ Date: _____

Format

My essay is in the correct format (title centered, first line of every paragraph
   indented, margins on both sides, double spaced). ☐ yes ☐ no

Content and Organization

My essay fits the assignment. I expressed my opinion on a controversial topic. ☐ yes ☐ no

Introduction

The general statements in my introductory paragraph explain the problem or issue. ☐ yes ☐ no

The last sentence of my introduction is my thesis statement, in which
   I tell my opinion. (Copy the thesis statement.) ☐ yes ☐ no

_____

Body

The body has _____ paragraphs. (*Write a number.*)

In each body paragraph, I support my opinion with a different reason. ☐ yes ☐ no

I used examples, statistics, and quotations to support my reasons. (*How many of each?*) ☐ yes ☐ no
   Examples _____ Statistics _____ Quotations _____

Conclusion

In my conclusion, I (*check one*) ☐ summarized my reasons ☐ repeated my thesis in different words

Unity

Each paragraph discusses only one reason, and there are no sentences that
   are off the topic. ☐ yes ☐ no

Coherence

Each paragraph flows smoothly from beginning to end. ☐ yes ☐ no

I repeat key nouns and pronouns ☐ yes ☐ no

I use transition signals to show relationships among ideas. ☐ yes ☐ no

I use transition signals to link paragraphs. ☐ yes ☐ no

Punctuation, Capitalization, and Spelling

I checked my punctuation, capitalization, and spelling. ☐ yes ☐ no

Grammar and Sentence Structure

I varied my sentence structure by writing simple, compound, and complex sentences. ☐ yes ☐ no

I checked my paragraph for fragments, comma splices, and run-ons. ☐ yes ☐ no

Personal Grammar Trouble Spots

**Number found
and corrected**

I checked my paragraph for _____ errors. _____
                        (verb tense, article, etc.)

I checked my paragraph for _____ errors. _____

I checked my paragraph for _____ errors. _____

Index